2015

RING IN THE DESERT

Sayyar Ismail Swift

HAQ OVER BATIL

1/1/2015

TABLE OF CONTENTS

Written and compiled in Casablanca, Morocco

English, French & Arabic Translation © Copyright

Copy Right 2014 © Sayyar Isma'l Swift First Edition (1st Edition)...

Order and fan based Email: ....haqoverbatil@gmail.com

Edited by: .... Sayyar Isma'il Swift

Corrections: .... Sayyar Isma'il Swift

Art:... Mrs. Nezha Mosleh & Sayyar Isma'il Swift

Printed: .... USA, Canada & North Africa

<u>PREVIOUS WORK</u>

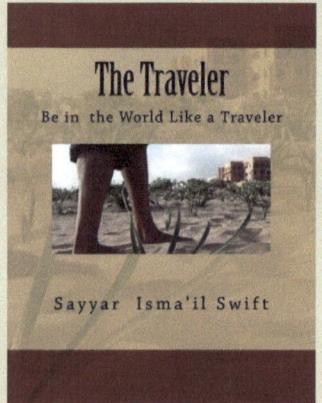

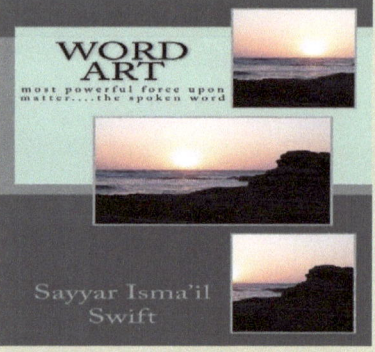

"Semantics" *(new poetry release)*

We all want the same things...differences should hinder us instead they should compel us to get to know each other...

Authored by Mr. Sayyar Ismail Swift

Politically correct or just Semantics? We all want the same things in life...differences should not hinder us; instead they should compel to know one another...

For those of you who seek debate... I don't like to enter debate for the simple reason of the very nature of debate...reason/logic is often over-stepped and the participants often focus on their own tradition, emotion & tactics to out speak, confuse, or ask mundane questions while they themselves are just fishing for knowledge. I have learned you can't reason with arrogance nor can you with closed hearts & minds opposed to the truth or bent on their own misunderstanding. Interpretations of the rich Semitic language really doesn't do any justice and the miracle that lies in the words of the creator can't be conveyed...it's solely up to the individual to learn the language then the lord will speak directly to you, which is what he wants anyway. However, I do fall victim to deeply wanting to share the beauty of the truth and then find myself on the other side of ignorance in defense of myself, but nothing speaks louder than hard core facts.The tongue behind an ego seeking to legitimize itself is something very dangerous...I write for the simple pleasure of education and knowledge sharing. I don't speak from my own opinion ON facts, but at other times if and when I do, I state it's my opinion so the reader will know. We are accountable for what we put out...therefore I take my task very serious. I have never run from anyone, and Insha'Allah Allah keep me strong to never do so in the future...but I'm also mature enough to gracefully bow out of a senseless word volley.

I would love to share all the knowledge that I have and also learn things I don't know from anyone who possess that information. I share my writing not from a biased positioned because I believe the truth has its own bias as does falsehood. I have tackled other topics in my 1st book "<u>Where does the Truth Begin</u>":

- Religion
- Jewish tribes amongst the inhabitants of Medina awaiting the advent of the prophet which Isa ibn Mariam a.s. prophesied would be a descendant of Isma'il whom they knew was settled in the desert land of Mt. Paran also known to be Mecca and Medina valley.
- Translation of Semitic languages, and interpretation
- Message of all the prophets, differences in Messengers and prophets (Rasool & Nabi) and other related issues.

I addressed some other topics of concern here, so if I generalized on some points that may have arose questions within you, I encourage you to read that book. I don't hold all the answers, nor have I or maybe I never will address every topic; I try to promote thought instead and offer a link to the truth…I never try to rob anyone of their personal responsibilities of seeking the truth. So much information is out there defining the truth…and there's also much in negative attribution trying to keep the truth mired or socially unacceptable; you must not allow these things to blind you…

I would be more than happy to answer any questions pertaining to the content of what you will read here, so don't hesitate to email me haqoverbatil@gmail.com

Prophet Muhammad s.a.w. mentioned in the bible

It is mentioned in the book of Isaiah chapter 29 verse 12:

"And the book is delivered to him that is not learned, saying, Read this, I pray thee: and he saith, I am not learned." When Archangel Gabriel commanded Muhammad (pbuh) by saying Iqra - "Read", he replied, "I am not learned".

Almighty God speaks to Moses in Book of Deuteronomy chapter 18 verse 18:

"I will raise them up a Prophet from among their brethren, like unto thee, and I will put my words in his mouth; and he shall speak unto them all that I shall command him."

The Christians say that this prophecy refers to Jesus (pbuh) because Jesus (pbuh) was like Moses (pbuh). Moses (pbuh) was banu Israel, as well as Jesus (pbuh) was from banu Israel; Moses (pbuh) was a Prophet and Jesus (pbuh) was also a Prophet.

If these two are the only criteria for this prophecy to be fulfilled, then all the Prophets of the Bible who came after Moses (pbuh) such as Solomon, Isaiah, Ezekiel, Daniel, Hosea, Joel, Malachi, John the Baptist, etc. (pbut) will fulfill this prophecy since all were banu israel as well as prophets.

However, it is Prophet Muhammad (pbuh) who is like Moses (pbuh):

> i) Both had a father and a mother, while Jesus (pbuh) was born miraculously without any male intervention.
>
> [Mathew 1:18 and Luke 1:35 and also Al-Qur'an 3:42-47]
>
> ii) Both were married and had children. Jesus (pbuh) according to the Bible did not marry nor had children.
>
> iii) Both died natural deaths. Jesus (pbuh) has been raised up alive. (4:157-158)
>
> Muhammad (pbuh) is from among the brethren of Moses (pbuh). Arabs are brethren of banu israel. Abraham (pbuh) had two sons: Ishmael and Isaac (pbut). The Arabs are the descendants of Ishmael (pbuh) and the banu israel are the descendants of Isaac (pbuh).
>
> Words in the mouth:
>
> Prophet Muhammad (pbuh) was unlettered and whatever revelations he received from Almighty God he repeated them verbatim.
>
> "I will raise them up a Prophet from among their brethren, like unto thee, and will put my words in his mouth; and he shall speak unto them all that I shall command him."
>
> [Deuteronomy 18:18]
>
> iv) Both besides being Prophets were also kings i.e. they could inflict capital punishment. Jesus (pbuh) said,"My kingdom is not of this world." (John 18:36).
>
> v) Both were accepted as Prophets by their people in their lifetime but Jesus (pbuh) was rejected by his people. John chapter 1 verse 11 states, "He came unto his own, but his own received him not."

iv) Both brought new laws and new regulations for their people. Jesus (pbuh) according to the Bible did not bring any new laws. (Mathew 5:17-18).

"Nevertheless I tell you the truth; it is expedient for you that I go away: for if I go not away, the Comforter will not come unto you; but if I depart, I will send him unto you".

"Ahmed" or "Muhammad" meaning "the one who praises" or "the praised one" is almost the translation of the **Greek word** *Peryklytos*. In the Gospel of John 14:16, 15:26, and 16:7. The word 'Comforter' is used in the English translation for the Greek word **Paraclete which means advocate or a kind friend rather than a comforte**r. *Paraclete* is the warped reading for *Peryklytos*. Jesus (pbuh); actually prophesised "Ahmed" by name… Even the Greek word *Paraclete* refers to the Prophet (pbuh) who is a mercy for all creatures.

Don't openly & readily deny this linguistic fact…to take revelation in English as ultimate truth is a fallacy since it was never revealed in that language…secondly, the English is derived from the Greek translation so to get a better understanding of the meaning you must refer back to it…then ultimately back to Semitic language laws of singularity, plural, and royal "WE" of Power…

Some Christians say that the Comforter mentioned in these prophecies refers to the Holy Spirit. They fail to realise that the prophecy clearly says that only if Jesus (pbuh) departs will the Comforter come. The Bible states that the Holy Spirit was already present on earth before and during the time of Jesus (pbuh), in the womb of Elizabeth, and again when Jesus (pbuh) was being baptised, etc. Hence this prophecy refers to none other than Prophet Muhammad (pbuh).

With every prophet of Allah with their respective messages and guidance Allah bestowed on them a miracle to accompany them and validate their authority as prophets…We know of all of the most famous of miracles from Moses and Jesus…The people who witnessed those miracles in enhanced their faith 1000 fold; and upon that miracle they had no more reasons to doubt, with the exception of a few. Now, you and I today haven't witnessed these same miracles, so our faith is therefore left to the individual effort and the mercy of our lord. The previous miracles were something for the eye to behold which affected the heart…the stories of those miracles have been disseminated through the generations. But is your faith today the same as those who actually saw the miracle? No, not even close…

Well, I want to tell you that one more miracle exist…Quran!!! Unlike the miracle that can only be witnessed with the eye, which if you aren't around to see it you miss…The Quran is the miracle that is perceived through the ear. Timeless…Big deal you might say! Well the beauty of this miracle is that it can be witnessed by every generation, and not just upon the generation present at the time of the prophet. But, there's a catch…the miracle of the Qur'an lies in the Arabic language in which it was revealed. The Quran is revelation, legislation, administration, and it's a miracle all within itself. The messages of our Lord were always meant to be read in the word in which he revealed them so that you receive the true benefit, and then the Lord will be communicating direct with his slave (you and I) as it is intended. This enhances the spiritual experience we have with our creator; Translation is not revelation; this unparalleled fact is undeniable and offers no rebuttal but only to the one who is stubborn in accepting the truth. The essence of religion in what one will come to believe in is preserved by authentic language. Humanity would be in a different place of accordance had they sought to preserve the languages of previous revelations…but the sackers and evil-doers attacked this particular aspect knowingly that by & through this effort they would be able to distort the truth…

Bismi-allah Ar'Rahman Ar'Rahim wa mursalan elay Rasoolullah salallahu alahi wa salaam wa alaa A'aleehi wa a'sahabihi thaweAtuwqa…

I begin with the name of Allah (Creator of heavens & earth) the Beneficent and most Merciful and by sending blessings of peace upon the last Messenger/Prophet Muhammad his family, companions and all Prophets from Adam to Muhammad & every believer until the last day.

Y

OKED ربط

Together In Burden & Punishment…, blind followers and those who had followers

(Trendsetters; in misleading ideas, doctrine, celebrity, idol worship and their followers)

Appearances Strategy (what's the truth beyond all the confusion)…

INTRODUCTION

Each of us has an innate desire to trust; but in a world such as this when lies are uttered so frequently, with straight-faces people take it as the truth; it makes life very hard. Everyone has become actors and actresses...spies of one another; it makes dropping out or seeking altered states of mind a weekly craving. Who do you trust, where do you turn? Even personal matters have been duped in betrayal, creating a selfish, everyone is out for there's dog eats dog world. Insight & investigation into matters is now required for everything...

I have heard many people address the topic of organized religion and the decisions to walk away from this type of controlling factor that harbors upon the moral campus of how one should live...This idea of taking people out of the occult of religion as a whole and introduce it as science, mainly that of evolution.

I agree the world is in a mess and the 3'major organized religions are especially at the worst they've ever been...but that's precisely it!!! That particular tactic of causing so much confusion and misinformation through media, has led some people to reach political breakdown...

Like torture; the subject undergoing the applied pain will say virtually anything to get the pain to STOP...and this is what appears to be on the minds of many they just want the pain of frustration and repeated words to stop...it's a sense of driving one to insanity...

They spare no expense to redundantly bombard the mindset of the masses with negative imagery and vocabulary hour after hour...Anderson cooper, then again with Wolfe Blitzer not to mention local news and radio...we live in an age of pausing live television, recording devices and Internet...why do we then need to be feed disinformation so frequently on the hour? Well, it's not a curtesy for those who may have missed a broadcast; instead it's a psychological tool being applied through the news and other programs by utilizing or adapting into it some of the vocabulary used to instill fear & other emotions.

If you have been one who has been guided to thinking that aliens created mankind, or we evolve from apes, or the holy books and superior knowledge of antiquity came from alien presence on earth, or the elite created religion to control the masses, or you failed to pick up a dictionary to find out the meaning of this new onslaught of Arabic words used in media today...then you have already fell into the trap. These same people think they are better off in the grey area, but as you will come to know, politics is just one side of this trap...the true trap is your soul. These events are mired in secrets, and you must come to be aware of that.

This is taking place especially in the western countries to keep the public sold on the affairs of the government internationally...Why? Because you are supposedly a democracy; and by that you have the power to stir the government to a consensus reflecting public decision. But is that the case? Are the citizens effectively able to alter the direction of their government?

I would surely suggest that if that power of the people still exist; I would quickly add that that power is readily diminishing, and it's only a means now of deferred action to a persistent agenda of world leaders using the American military to carry out it plans.

People are growing very tired of war and so the concept of a global army is being brought about, which is the real idea behind NATO... This new world army, will offer the idea that no more war can take place because there's only one army, but it is a diluted, diverse fact of control of the entire world all managed by Israel and the last anti-Christ. This is the deception behind Israel's plight of playing the victim by controlling the media of what the world see's and a tactic of trying to win and keep the support of blinded individuals & countries in their aide...

These designated predictions were made early on just after the turn of the millennium by a prominent masonic figure and since these predictions the path of events have followed one by one. This includes the induced Arab spring that would bring about the concluding consensus of most people in the Middle East for a caliphate and at the same time be used to scare the world and help Israel to appear the feeble, humble victim surrounded by this horrible fate if not aided. This is the truth behind the fiction and delivery of information by newly created ethnic news media stations by American corporate stations like CNN affiliation channel to Al-Jazeera for the Arab world; its role in stirring the masses as a sort of double agent with giving some truth mixed with a lot of lies...

It's crystal clear and these analyses have all had huge consensuses amongst scholars, and political theorist and their likes...

The idea behind democracy is free minds collectively working together to blanket all wants and desire of the people and to have those things represented in their government; not a collective mass following of tyranny and guided thought...

You see, the infiltration of organized religion took place long, long ago and all have been tainted dramatically, especially with lost original scripture of Jews and Christians... It's virtually now a doctrine of political control towards an apocalyptic outcome; hence this final prophesied clash of civilizations.

C OMMUNICATION

Held to the peripheral intake of information primarily through the eyes, then the ears...the public can very easily be deceived of truth. Many things have been omitted or added, and even completely hidden from general public knowledge altogether. History itself speaks to this point...

Since no one reads anymore they have put their trust of information into the hands of individuals who are deliberating stirring mankind to a very bad ending.

Communication is the basis of all civilization...trust, business & other bonds are built through this medium; the efficiency of a society, the justice of a society, the neighborhood, city, state & government all reflect this one device that's so critical to the longevity of our existence.

Dissemination of wrong information is essentially the worst kind of communication; criminal in fact because it often leads to death of innocent people as we unfortunately see every day in the news or some other media conveyance. Instead of coping out of the political jargon arena of constant chatter, we need to learn how to tune into the truth and or research information before becoming another channel that is used to further convey the wrong information. The truth is out there in abundance, it's shrouded in all sorts of disguises and unmarked coverings that you have to delve into a little before it becomes obvious and clear. One uniquely acute trait about the truth is, when a person hears it the subconscious can't get enough of it and we often remain over taken while it pours out onto us; but the conscious self the one that is influenced by outside stimuli, prejudices, arrogance, traditions and cultures...regains hold and motions us back to old ways and feelings. This is something that has to be understood and confronted by all; the heart and mind have to be clear in order to receive information and to process that information correctly.

The first thing someone's says about fighting is learning how to control your anger, and exercise the adult manner of walking away...well this is really no different...the self has to be able control itself in regards to prejudices & preferences to receive what it is undertaking otherwise it falls on deaf ears so to speak...

Information is all around us! Understanding that most communication is non-verbal...most of the information that is taken in is by eyesight mans most trusted and followed asset...and this particular METHOD of informing the masses is used as a propaganda weapon To condition public opinion and ultimately your overall viewpoints which today have become global.

Friends & Family

Take a good look around you...how many childhood friends do you still have? From them, if any, are they pretty much unchanged besides just aging a bit? Same with the family; how many have changed? What I mean by change is self-progression. Have their lifestyles change, ambitions, aspiration, and the big one, strength of inner self seen in the way they carry themselves? A sliding scale for each of us; not playing God in judging anyone; but observing what it outwardly manifested. In my case, I have less than 5 childhood friends that remain friends with me today, and very few family members I'm in touch with on a regular basis. My younger brother because he's my beloved brother and his son I speak to often, but my oldest brother & my father we barely speak. I make an effort too but it's not successful. I mean you can't force someone to talk to you right? When I do speak with them there's a sort of dead silence but with speech, if you understand what I mean. You can tell the other person is searching for things to say instead of a conversation naturally progressing. The weather, food dishes, job are sustained until they're bled dry of information then I find myself only answering questions after that. The other person is now deliberating asking questions, and while I respond, I suppose they aren't really listening genuinely, but instead prepping for the next question as it flies out after I finish. I sometimes play along and return those same questions if its relevant, and then I can feel Them squirming trying to avoid the same onslaught of questions and trying to regain control of the conversation.

Not too good at what they do, and I most often passively humble myself just to have some sort of communication with them. But why is the situation like this? How did things ever get to this point? What have I done to deserve to be treated in this manner? From one aspect I understand not much has changed for them in comparison to what they may be thinking in regards to me since I'm always traveling, but what happen to honestly, and integrity. What happened to personal integrity an acceptance of your own individual fates? After all choices you and I make have helped to shape the environments around ourselves. I know that my experiences are amazing and rare compared to the average person, and although I may get excited at times to convey or share those experiences I am also aware and try not to overdo it because I know jealousies exist even amongst family. I guess this is where I am in my life...caught between the rock of love and hard place of envies...

I find it appropriate to share with you from this perceptive because communication and relationships have been penetrated not just between common folk in our day to day lives outside the home; but the vices employed to sow this dissension have come into our home through the television, radio and Internet and it has changed the mindsets between family members even. I find it quite disturbing and a complete violation and oxymoron of hypocrisy in the speech of some trying to win an audience in justifying some political motive.

When I use the term "politic", I'm not always referring to government; instead I use the term also to define individual rhetoric of just talk without action of sincere meaning...

It is now only those homes in which do not subscribe to ownership of a television, and if the Internet is in the home it's monitored and used under supervision. If the parents today aren't the best friends to their children then they will be at risk of being swept away in the mind control propaganda of conditioned thinking and synergy of falsehood based information towards a satanic existence in this new world order.

However, with a friendship between parent and child the level of respect and discipline need not weaken. It's not appropriate for a parent to alter the wrongs and rights based on a new age kind of thinking as if wrongs are progressed rights with changes in modernity. It's also definitely not cool for parents to drink, or get high with their children because no matter the age respect can be altered or circumstances can arise during this indulged state that aren't appropriate for child and parent to undertake, discuss, or deal with. Morals, Values & modesty are never out-done or out dated as is being taught today...shamelessness and lack thereof are a reflection of faith...and if someone lives without consideration to their actions whatsoever this is a person who has no fear of what he/she will be accountable for...

W*AR*

Not since the cold war has media propaganda been used so effectively and abundantly on the populace of peoples than it's being used today...the world is at the cusp of another major turning point in history where Israel becomes the ruling state in the world at the controlled, systematic collapse of the united states. You say, what makes you so sure about this statement? Well, it's part of prophecy...part of Israel's becoming the ruling state gives legitimacy to the anti-Christ who will emerge & assume power claiming to be the messiah...the prophet said the Ad'Dajjal would live on earth for 40 days; __1__days like a year, then _1__days like a month then 1 day like a week and finally the rest of his days like our days and this is the time he will appear in and live amongst us. Now each one of these transitions also coincide with power shifts in the world from: Caliphate of Ottoman rule under which represented the rule of Divine law carried over for centuries from the last prophet s.a.w...to Britain (*who establishes rule of law by man*), then America (*who establishes separation church & state as well as NATO*), and then finally Israel...we all know that under British rule after the fall of the Caliphate, Britain helped to establish many kingships in the middle east after they carved up the middle east with the **Sykes–Picot Agreement** between Britain and France… as well as the Zionist movement pushing for a state in Palestine(*to be called "Israel"*)for the European Jews. Upholding their part of the deal from Jewish help of bringing America into the war on the side of the British; never was there a land named Israel, until 1947-48 which was one of the major accomplishments of the false occupiers of this area. These same accomplishments of the past are paving the way politically today to the accomplishment of a ruling state from Jerusalem.

You have to ask yourself, after listening to all the speeches of the Israeli president and America's unyielding support of the Jewish state, why? Why are they so certain that their actions are correct? Well, it satisfies their beliefs towards the false messiah as a prophecy soon fulfilled; because only when Israel is the ruling state will the last and final anti-Christ take his place among men as foretold by our beloved Nabi Muhammad s.a.w. *(read other chapters for details outlining this issue)*.

This is the Real motivation behind Israeli *(Judeo-Christian alliances since the crusades and now with evangelical mega-churches all calling and contributing funds to support Israel)* politics...

During each stage of Western rule, the currency has been taken over by the ruling state of each becoming the international reserve currency effectively controlling the money of the world. Intrinsic wealth has since then been slowly transformed to fiat paper currency without any real value backing the notes of receipt people actually hold. Dinar & Dirham shifted to the sterling pound, and then shifted to the USA dollar...which today, is suspended by OPEC holding its sales in the dollar for purchase of oil. "Whoever controls the resources does in fact control the world"…until the pending but inevitable collapse of all paper money. America has shared her debt with all nations by forcing them to carry the USA $ for purchases of oil since the 1970's…thus all paper money will collapse with her. This will bring about the culmination of an age of electronic money which is already upon us. With this the control of people is absolute, because money is no longer tangible or intrinsic...instead it's digits typed into an account with your name that can be just as easily seized as it is allowed to function on your behalf. This notion is also highly in alignment with the writings of Albert Pike's book outlining the three major conflicts of all world wars' including the 3rd, which is brewing now and how they would be brought about. This is beyond coincidence and deserves your full attention if you are still ignorant of these collaborating facts. I will only mention a few:

Sahih Muslim in "The Book Pertaining to the Turmoil and Portents of the Last Hour"

(Kitab Al-Fitan wa Ashrat As-Sa'ah)

Anas b. Malik reported that **Allah's Messenger** (May peace be upon him) said:

There would be written three letters k. f. r., i. e. Kafir, between the eyes of the *Dajjal.*

"حَدَّثَنَا ابْنُ الْمُثَنَّى، وَابْنُ، بَشَّار ـ وَاللَّفْظُ لِابْنِ الْمُثَنَّى ـ قَالَا حَدَّثَنَا مُعَاذُ بْنُ هِشَامٍ، حَدَّثَنِي أَبِي، عَنْ قَتَادَة، حَدَّثَنَا أَنَسُ بْنُ مَالِكٍ، أَنَّ نَبِيَّ اللهِ صلى الله عليه وسلم قَالَ الدَّجَّالُ مَكْتُوبٌ بَيْنَ عَيْنَيْهِ كـ فـ رأى كَافِرٌ"

The Arabic word kfr (kafir) which means disbeliever on the forehead between the eyes similar to the swastika on Charles Manson forehead (in the photo) who is recognized as one of the 30 minor anti-Christ claiming to be Messiah Esa Ibn Mariam a.s

It's ironic to learn that Israel recently formed The **Kfir Brigade** (Hebrew: חֲטִיבַת כְּפִיר, also known as **900 Brigade**, is the youngest infantry brigade of the Israel Defense Forces. It is subordinate to the 162nd Division of Israel's Central Regional Command. The brigade is currently deployed in the West Bank where its *primary missions include counter-terror operations, apprehension of Palestinian terrorists, patrols, manning checkpoints and regular security activities.*

Sahih Muslim "The Book Pertaining to the Turmoil and Portents of the Last Hour"
(Kitab Al-Fitan wa Ashrat As-Sa'ah)

Anas b. Malik reported that **Allah's Messenger** (may peace be upon him) said:

The *Dajjal* would be followed by seventy thousand Jews of Isfahan (Iran) wearing Persian shawls.

يَتْبَعُ "حَدَّثَنَا مَنْصُورُ بْنُ أَبِي مُزَاحِمٍ، حَدَّثَنَا يَحْيَى بْنُ حَمْزَة، عَنِ الأَوْزَاعِيِّ، عَنْ إِسْحَاقَ، بْنِ عَبْدِ اللهِ أَنَّ رَسُولَ اللهِ صلى الله عليه وسلم قَالَ أَنَس، بْنِ مَالِكٍ عَنْ عَمِّهِ، الدَّجَّالَ مِنْ يَهُودِ أَصْبَهَانَ سَبْعُونَ أَلْفًا عَلَيْهِمُ الطَّيَالِسَةُ"

Many people don't understand the obsession of Israel with Iran; in particular the city of Isfahan...Isfahan just so happens to be the location of the so called nuclear reactor of Iran; and it's no secret about the nearly 70,000 Jews that currently lives there. These are not fabricated stories of mere coincidences of political likeness that should be shrugged off as most people treat these issues; but instead these are factual events taking place and or soon will take place and it's all prophecy that you can find authentically documented from our lords last prophet Muhammad s.a.w..

Jami' at-Tirmidhi Chapters on "Al-Fitan"
Abu Hurairah narrated that the **Messenger of Allah** (s.a.w) said:

"The Hour shall not be established until nearly thirty imposters, *Dajjal* appear, each of them claiming that he is the Messenger of Allah."

لَا تَقُومُ السَّاعَةُ حَتَّى يَنْبَعِثَ "حَدَّثَنَا مَحْمُودُ بْنُ غَيْلَانَ، حَدَّثَنَا عَبْدُ الرَّزَّاقِ، أَخْبَرَنَا مَعْمَرٌ، عَنْ هَمَّامِ بْنِ مُنَبِّهٍ، عَنْ أَبِي هُرَيْرَة، قَالَ قَالَ رَسُولُ اللهِ صلى الله عليه وسلم قَالَ أَبُو عِيسَى وَفِي الْبَابِ عَنْ جَابِرِ بْنِ سَمُرَةَ وَابْنِ عُمَرَ . وَهَذَا حَدِيثٌ حَسَنٌ صَحِيحٌ "دَجَّالُونَ كَذَّابُونَ قَرِيبٌ مِنْ ثَلَاثِينَ كُلُّهُمْ يَزْعُمُ أَنَّهُ رَسُولُ اللهِ

This points to all of the many occult and leaders of countries that have impacted humanity after the time of the prophet…they fit this prophecy.

The likes of in no particular order: Napoleon, Hitler, Stalin, The cult leader in South America who killed his Christian followers by poison, Nostradamus, already mentioned Charles Manson etc…

Jami' at-Tirmidhi Chapters On "Al-Fitan"
Abu Bahriyyah, a Companion of Mu'adh bin Jabal narrated that **the Prophet** (s.a.w) said:

"The great Malhamah {(apocalyptic war)}, the conquest of Constantinople, and the coming of the ***Dajjal*** occur in (the span of) seven months."

حَدَّثَنَا عَبْدُ اللَّهِ بْنُ عَبْدِ الرَّحْمَنِ، أَخْبَرَنَا الْحَكَمُ بْنُ الْمُبَارَكِ، حَدَّثَنَا الْوَلِيدُ بْنُ مُسْلِمٍ، عَنْ أَبِي بَكْرِ بْنِ أَبِي مَرْيَمَ، عَنِ الْوَلِيدِ بْنِ سُفْيَانَ، عَنْ يَزِيدَ بْنِ قُطَيْبٍ السَّكُونِيِّ، عَنْ
قَالَ أَبُو " الْمَلْحَمَةُ الْعُظْمَى وَفَتْحُ الْقُسْطَنْطِينِيَّةِ وَخُرُوجُ الدَّجَّالِ فِي سَبْعَةِ أَشْهُرٍ "أَبِي بَحْرِيَّةَ، صَاحِبِ مُعَاذِ بْنِ جَبَلٍ، عَنِ النَّبِيِّ صلى الله عليه وسلم قَالَ
عِيسَى وَفِي الْبَابِ عَنِ الصَّعْبِ بْنِ جَثَّامَةَ وَعَبْدِ اللَّهِ بْنِ بُسْرٍ وَعَبْدِ اللَّهِ بْنِ مَسْعُودٍ وَأَبِي سَعِيدٍ الْخُدْرِيِّ . وَهَذَا حَدِيثٌ حَسَنٌ غَرِيبٌ لاَ نَعْرِفُهُ إِلاَّ مِنْ هَذَا الْوَجْهِ .

The Great Malhamah was told would begin with a war in Iraq; then be a series of small conflicts all over the world that would lead to the "Great War". We have been witnessing these events for many years now, and America and her allies have been spearheading the efforts. You have to understand the Jewish influence and power over the USA government; when you do then you will understand the use of the American military and your tax dollars all to prop up the true conspirators; In the meantime they try to maintain their innocent mannerisms although I think by now people are becoming to know the evils behind Israeli motives…

Constantinople is current day Istanbul, Turkey…this prophecy has yet to come; however it explains all the current politics directed at the old Soviet States made by NATO. The agenda of NATO to absorb these States, and the coup and government take-over of Ukraine are all done in the understanding of the importance of Constantinople (Istanbul). This city is strategically important because of the canal and pathway from the Black Sea into the Mediterranean Sea. The Russian fleet in Syria and their access in these water ways are all surrounding this particular city; which Russia counters American aggression in the Ukraine with the treaty and absorption of Crimea. These are the motives surrounding this ahadith of the Nabi Muhammad s.a.w…

Jami' at-Tirmidhi Chapters On Al-Fitan
Mujammi' bin Jariyah Al-Ansari said:

"I heard the Messenger of Allah (s.a.w) saying: 'Eisa bin Maryam (Jesus son of Mary) will kill the ***Dajjal*** at the gate of Ludd.'"

حَدَّثَنَا قُتَيْبَةُ، حَدَّثَنَا اللَّيْثُ، عَنِ ابْنِ شِهَابٍ، عَنْ سَمِعَ عُبَيْدَ اللَّهِ بْنَ عَبْدِ اللَّهِ بْنِ ثَعْلَبَةَ الأَنْصَارِيَّ، يُحَدِّثُ عَنْ عَبْدِ الرَّحْمَنِ بْنِ يَزِيدَ بْنِ الأَنْصَارِيِّ، مِنْ بَنِي عَمْرِو بْنِ عَوْفٍ
قَالَ وَفِي الْبَابِ عَنْ عِمْرَانَ " يَقْتُلُ ابْنُ مَرْيَمَ الدَّجَّالَ بِبَابِ لُدٍّ "يَقُولُ سَمِعْتُ رَسُولَ مُجَمِّعِ بْنِ جَارِيَةَ الأَنْصَارِيِّ يَقُولُ سَمِعْتُ عَمِّي، اللَّهِ صلى الله عليه وسلم يَقُولُ
بْنِ حُصَيْنٍ وَنَافِعِ بْنِ عُتْبَةَ وَأَبِي بَرْزَةَ وَحُذَيْفَةَ بْنِ أَسِيدٍ وَأَبِي هُرَيْرَةَ وَكَيْسَانَ وَعُثْمَانَ بْنِ أَبِي الْعَاصِي وَجَابِرٍ وَأَبِي أُمَامَةَ وَابْنِ مَسْعُودٍ وَعَبْدِ اللَّهِ بْنِ عَمْرٍو وَسَمُرَةَ بْنِ
جُنْدَبٍ وَالنَّوَّاسِ بْنِ سَمْعَانَ وَعَمْرِو بْنِ عَوْفٍ وَحُذَيْفَةَ بْنِ الْيَمَانِ . قَالَ أَبُو عِيسَى هَذَا حَدِيثٌ حَسَنٌ صَحِيحٌ .

Ad'Dajjal is a man, but the empirical culmination of evil; Satan's earthly emissary who will poses powers of magic aided by the jinn etc. and permitted by our Lord as a Fitnah (trial) on the people; similar to the fitnah of Harut & Marut (the twin Angels sent by the Lord to try the faith) on the people in Babylon. This will cause many people to accept him as divine deity; the Messiah… much like the way people believe in Jesus as a deity. The True Messiah descends from the heavens, where this imposer, deceiver will emerge from the East (Isfahan)…

One of the last encounters before the end of the Dajjal is his seeing Eisa bin Mariam as his army prepares a last assault and stand against the Muslim army in which Eisa bin Mariam will be a part along with the Caliph of Imam Mahdi and direct descendant of Muhammad s.a.w and is also prophesized to come along with the return of the Caliphate of divine law in governing…Upon his seeing the true Messiah his skin begins to dissolve like salt does in water; So, he flees and Eisa bin Mariam gives chase. He catches up to Ad 'Dajjal at the gate of Ludd, which also happens to be near an airport (not visible in photo). He kills the false Messiah anti-Christ, and the people upon seeing this believe in the True Messiah Eisa bin Mariam a.s.

Figure 1 LUDD ISRAEL

This is all documented, factual, PROPHECY…not just some made up fairy-tale for you to enjoy in reading. These are the events and the agenda of our world leaders today. League of Nations yesterday, today NATO…the World Wide Web, one world army, and one world government disguised with the return of the Zionist Messiah Ad 'Dajjal…

All sorts of movements have popped up to inform the populace of people about hidden information or motives, but unfortunately this information has been gathered well after the fact…and they have moved on to higher orders of bringing about what they ultimately want. Nonetheless, it's a great service for those doing so to inform, as I myself try to do the same, however political alignment is only a fraction of what is taking place.

The movements of the entertainment industry, business (which encompasses finance/economy which also affects the education sector) governments, current wars, and upcoming events you will find all rooted in a religious campaign; politics is only the means used to stir and control these agendas… **Novus ordo seclorum** this is the project of stripping the entire world of faith base religions to the new order which will harbor satanic belief; a world stripped of God and belief. Now if you keep that thought on the forefront of your mind and bring it to consideration when you're tuned into the news and other media hopefully it will shed some light to the disguise. The USA and its allies are trying to be very clever in their true efforts and in doing so you will never hear them say they are at war with Islam. This is for a couple of reasons, *#1 it goes against the very fabric of the founding ideas of the country and constitution…freedom of religion and other bills of rights #2 in making such a claim, they would be responsible for a world-wide response of unifying 1.6 billion Muslims. This is the main reason you see pockets of conflict all disguised in political rhetoric with media propaganda to help confuse the people towards the truth.* Everywhere around the world in recent news Muslims called rebels for political news coverage, have been attacked in India, Kashmir, Burma, Philippines, china, Chechnya, Africa and of course the middle east.

Islam has been so well campaigned against that the ignorance of truth about Islam is completely buried under hate and deliberate attack. But if Washington and her friends spoke truthfully about their intentions then those who look through eyes of hatred from induced news and or ignorance of blind following, would quickly second guess theirs eyes at the mobilization of a billion plus Muslims. In my opinion, I fault Muslims today for the bad images people have adapted because for decades we have lived in countries not predominantly Muslim and have maintain a boundary both physically and verbally instead of mingling and disseminating the true message about Islam. This has given the media machine an advantage in teaching Islam from their poisonous perspective instead of its essence of peace. Now, Muslims are responding to negativity which instead of being perceived in good faith it is more so seen as a defense of faith and ideology.

Be it as it may, the world's remaining faithful need to eventually see that what is being slowly introduced goes against their own beliefs. One good means of measuring the effects of this new godless existence is by looking at the youth. Watch how they carry themselves, act out, socialize, speak, dress, actions, rebellion, and diminished faith...their campaign has already captured hundreds of thousands of youth world-wide.

After colonialism a new leash had to be implemented to rule by proxy and without a known presence...so the financial/economical trap was set.

1). **Fiat money** is currency which derives its value from government regulation or law; It differs from commodity money with intrinsic value, which is based on a good, often a precious metal such as gold or silver, which has uses other than exchange. Other items have been used for exchange such as: salt, frankincense, silk, dates, farm crops etc. All hold internal value therefore could be used to exchange for other goods...Today, money is printed based on debt...each time the US government pays on its loans they are left in need, which keeps them involved in the vicious cycle of pay and borrow. The successive recessions and export of manufacturing and other services expunging millions of jobs has left the USA with a GDP less than par, so in ways of increasing it's bottom-line to slowly chopped down the debt; they have been mired in the economic mud.

The credit addiction of Americans is prohibited in divine law which is also present in the bible: I list all occurrences to be thorough in making sure you understand...that includes all business of borrowing where interest is applied...So why do (any) people of faith deal in it?

- **Exodus 22:25** - If thou lend money to [any of] my people [that is] poor by thee, thou shalt not be to him as a usurer, neither shalt thou lay upon him usury.

    Ezekiel 18:13 - Hath given forth upon usury, and hath taken increase: shall he then live? He shall not live: he hath done all these abominations; he shall surely die; his blood shall be upon him.

    Ezekiel 22:12 - In thee have they taken gifts to shed blood; thou hast taken usury and increase, and thou hast greedily gained of thy neighbours by extortion, and hast forgotten me, saith the Lord GOD.

    Ezekiel 18:8 - He [that] hath not given forth upon usury, neither hath taken any increase, [that] hath withdrawn his hand from iniquity, hath executed true judgment between man and man,

    Deuteronomy 23:19 - Thou shalt not lend upon usury to thy brother; usury of money, usury of victuals, usury of anything that is lent upon usury:

    Ezekiel 18:17 - [That] hath taken off his hand from the poor, [that] hath not received usury nor increase, hath executed my judgments, hath walked in my statutes; he shall not die for the iniquity of his father, he shall surely live.

Leviticus 25:37 - Thou shalt not give him thy money upon usury, nor lend him thy victuals for increase.

Jeremiah 15:10 - Woe is me, my mother, that thou hast borne me a man of strife and a man of contention to the whole earth! I have neither lent on usury, nor men have lent to me on usury; [yet] every one of them doth curse me.

Proverbs 28:8 - He that by usury and unjust gain increaseth his substance, he shall gather it for him that will pity the poor.

Proverbs 22:7 - The rich ruleth over the poor, and the borrower [is] servant to the lender.

Deuteronomy 23:19-20 - Thou shalt not lend upon usury to thy brother; usury of money, usury of victuals, usury of anything that is lent upon usury:
Nehemiah 5:1-13 - And there was a great cry of the people and of their wives against their brethren the Jews.
Leviticus 25:36 - Take thou no usury of him, or increase: but fear thy God; that thy brother may live with thee.

Psalms 15:5 - [He that] putteth not out his money to usury, nor taketh reward against the innocent. He that doeth these [things] shall never be moved.

Luke 6:35 - But love ye your enemies, and do good, and lend, hoping for nothing again; and your reward shall be great, and ye shall be the children of the Highest: for he is kind unto the unthankful and [to] the evil.

Matthew 25:27 - Thou oughtest therefore to have put my money to the exchangers, and [then] at my coming I should have received mine own with usury.

Psalms 15:1-5 - (A Psalm of David.) LORD, who shall abide in thy tabernacle? who shall dwell in thy holy hill?
Leviticus 25:35-37 - And if thy brother be waxen poor, and fallen in decay with thee; then thou shalt relieve him: [yea, though he be] a stranger, or a sojourner; that he may live with thee.

Acts 2:44-45 - And all that believed were together, and had all things common;

Isaiah 1:1-31 - The vision of Isaiah the son of Amoz, which he saw concerning Judah and Jerusalem in the days of Uzziah, Jotham, Ahaz, [and] Hezekiah, kings of Judah.
Nehemiah 5:1-19 - And there was a great cry of the people and of their wives against their brethren the Jews.

Deuteronomy 15:7-11 - If there be among you a poor man of one of thy brethren within any of thy gates in thy land which the LORD thy God giveth thee, thou shalt not harden thine heart, nor shut thine hand from thy poor brother:

Leviticus 25:1-55 - And the LORD spake unto Moses in mount Sinai, saying,
Matthew 25:1-46 - Then shall the kingdom of heaven be likened unto ten virgins, which took their lamps, and went forth to meet the bridegroom.
Isaiah 10:1-34 - Woe unto them that decree unrighteous decrees, and that write grievousness [which] they have prescribed;
Psalms 22:1-31 - (To the chief Musician upon Aijeleth Shahar, A Psalm of David.) My God, my God, why hast thou forsaken me? [why art thou so] far from helping me, [and from] the words of my roaring?
Hebrews 7:1-28 - For this Melchisedec, king of Salem, priest of the most high God, who met Abraham returning from the slaughter of the kings, and blessed him;

1 Timothy 2:9 - In like manner also, that women adorn themselves in modest apparel, with shamefacedness and sobriety; not with broided hair, or gold, or pearls, or costly array;

Galatians 5:3 - For I testify again to every man that is circumcised, that he is a debtor to do the whole law.

Acts 20:35 - I have shewed you all things, how that so labouring ye ought to support the weak, and to remember the words of the Lord Jesus, how he said, It is more blessed to give than to receive.

Luke 19:23 - Wherefore then gavest not thou my money into the bank, that at my coming I might have required mine own with usury?

Luke 19:1-48 - And [Jesus] entered and passed through Jericho.
Matthew 21:1-46 - And when they drew nigh unto Jerusalem, and were come to Bethphage, unto the mount of Olives, then sent Jesus two disciples,
Malachi 3:1-18 - Behold, I will send my messenger, and he shall prepare the way before me: and the Lord, whom ye seek, shall suddenly come to his temple, even the messenger of the covenant, whom ye delight in: behold, he shall come, saith the LORD of hosts.

Isaiah 50:1 - Thus saith the LORD, Where [is] the bill of your mother's divorcement, whom I have put away? Or which of my creditors [is it] to whom I have sold you? Behold, for your iniquities have ye sold yourselves, and for your transgressions is your mother put away.

I have explained this particular action in my 1st book entitled "**where does the truth begin**", which I hope educates the average person on the sciences of finance, politics and deviations in religion. However, in brief on finance, interest and interest rates are almost certain to exceed the amount of notes in circulation. When you come to know this then you also will understand that it's impossible to pay back loans with interest attached. In addition, to this the wealthy are constantly take money out of the rotation to hoard in the personal accounts. This leaves even lesser notes in circulation…this is why the economy needs stimulation by lowering the interest rates on loans so more people are tempted to borrow, which motivates spending.

The science of finance has to be understood, and then divine prohibitions obeyed & followed so you don't become a slave to debt…

2). Now since OPEC (oil producing exporting countries) are agreed to sell their oil in the USA currency this effectively has enable the USA to spread their debt to other countries while they in turn hand over there currency which may have goods backing the notes. This is no different than someone giving you a diamond and you returning to them just a plain rock with absolutely no value. This particular achievement of America in the **Brentwood's Accord**; and agreements made between the *Nixon administrations by Henry Kissinger with King Faisal of Saudi Arabia* has since then allowed the USA to print money based on the assumption of oil. They have removed all the gold and silver backing from USA notes and therefore the paper money is worthless.

The division of worlds 1st, 2nd, 3rd, has benefited the colonizers of the west by exploitation under colonialization and now by those countries thirst to join the ranks of the developed world in technology etc. This is the true idea and premise behind the pyramid structure that sucks from the lower ranks up to the fewer in the top.

Instead of standing guard over your captives they innovated ways to rule by proxy...

The political and financial leadership of underdeveloped countries to accept enormous development loans from institutions like the *World Bank and USAID*. Enticed to borrow with debts they could not hope to pay; those countries would be forced to acquiesce to political pressure from the United States on a variety of issues. Land grants for Naval ports, Military bases, Corporate cheaper labor, and or course access to the all so valuable natural resources...Its dirty dealing to the Nth power; I myself find it very shameful for a country and its leadership to wear two-faces as they do; but ultimately it's the fault of the people who remain ignorant to these conditions and or do nothing about it...

3). Economic hit men (EHMs) are highly paid professionals who cheat countries around the globe out of trillions of dollars. They funnel money from the **World Bank,** the **U.S. Agency for International Development (USAID),** and other foreign "aid" organizations into the coffers of huge corporations and the pockets of a few wealthy families who control the planet's natural resources.

Their tools included:

- **fraudulent financial reports**
- **rigged elections**
- **Payoffs**
- **Extortion**
- **Sex**
- **Murder**

They play a game as old as empire, but one that has taken on new and terrifying dimensions during this time of globalization.

The first real economic hit man was back in the early 1950s, Kermit Roosevelt, Jr., the grandson of Teddy, who overthrew the government of Iran, a democratically elected government, Mossadegh's government who was Time's magazine person of the year; and he was so successful at doing this without any bloodshed—well, there was a little bloodshed, but no military intervention, just spending millions of dollars and replaced Mossadegh with the Shah of Iran. At that point, we understood that this idea of economic hit man was an extremely good one. We didn't have to worry about the threat of war with Russia when we did it this way.

4).Corrupt leaders often proxies to western leaders; educated in secular knowledge and driven to the dirty deeds of appeasing the West often at the behest & murder of one's own people. The worst of people indeed…If the leadership in the Muslim world was together the invasion of Iraq would have not been possible. The lands, water ways and airspace were all given in agreement by many leaders in the area. Neither would the slaughters in Afghanistan, Bosnia, Kosovo, Kashmir, Chechnya, and Palestine have been possible if the Muslim rulers had their act together. But, this is by design and regarded against the people & their religion. Beamed around the world as backward, outdated, stone-aged and poor; while the western world is portrayed as civil.

But is this the fault of the 54 current so-called Muslim leaders; or are there more to blame? After all, these leaders aren't alone in governing the whole; they have obedient soldiers and armies, executive, judicial, and legislative branches who all help. Lastly, the people themselves have become watered down from deep seated values of integrity, honesty, and truthfulness. This has been the most powerful cause upon the corruption of leadership and the sustenance of decadence in this part of the world. Heavily, alienated in media and demographically targeting youth, education, economies, and modernity…religious campaigns disguised in fear of terrorism with the use of imagery against modesty; has even been effective against the people in their own cultures.

One of the most embarrassing of issues is WE Muslims have with us Allah/Gods last and final revelation the Quran, which confirms the Injeel (gospel of Esa bin Mariam), the Torah of Musa, and Zabur of Dawud (Prophet & King David)…it teaches us the best of actions and furthermore the best of deeds. Yet the Muslim world is shrined in embedded nationalism, language, and tribes, which brings about the idea of corruption not just in deed or actions but that of Ideas…This implication has far deeper implications because it's the facet that will depict deeds and actions themselves. In addition, more than likely it will be something passed down in heredity. We are taught the nation of muslims is one nation Dar-ul-Islam (the home of Islam) which has no boundaries and this was the condition under caliphate rule; anyone could travel from the Far East to west with no ordinances of passports etc. amongst the nations of Islam. There were no restrictions on travel, or movement of capital or goods. A Muslim could take up residence and start a business or get a job anywhere. Ibn Batuta (a famous muslim) traveled from Tunisia to Hijaz (Saudi Arabia mainly Mecca & Medina area), East Africa, India, Malaya, and China, covering 75000 miles without traveling the same road twice. During the twenty-five year journey he took up residence where he wanted to; got even government assignments as Qadi and even as ambassador in China for the Sultan in India.

Nationalism is a way of dividing people, and once divided they are then more easily conquered. It's a preference much like that of racism and it stinks in every since of the word…

Current affairs and events have solidified the fact that much of the Muslim world has bought into the idea of nationalism; and the view of leadership by less-action is an effective polling of the effectiveness of targeted manipulation and efforts made towards keeping the unity of a people scattered like sand in the wind. It's amazing what psychological tools of manipulation are able to do in decaying the integrity of people over time. The clash between Islam and the nation-state appears to all of us after the wars of Iraq and Afghanistan…Millions suffering yet bordering Muslim countries fail in their aide toward fellow Muslims. The strength of the Ummah was from its unity, and the blessing that comes with unity. The Quran warns the Muslims to not engage in infighting or the Ummah would become weak and powerless; is this not the case today?

Since the fall of the caliph...

SThe **Sykes–Picot Agreement**, officially known as the **Asia Minor Agreement**, was a secret agreement between the governments of the United Kingdom and France, with the assent of Russia; defining their proposed spheres of influence and control in the Middle East should the Triple Entente succeed in defeating the Ottoman Empire during World War I. The negotiation of the treaty occurred between November 1915 and March 1916. The agreement was concluded on 16 May 1916. The agreement effectively divided the Arab provinces of the Ottoman Empire outside the Arabian

Peninsula into areas of future British and French control or influence. The terms were negotiated by the French diplomat François Georges-Picot and Briton Sir Mark Sykes, which is attributed to them in naming the pact agreement. the Sykes–Picot Agreement becoming public only three weeks after the Balfour Declaration.

One very interesting note of literary history that has impacted the affairs of politics and events to the letter of its contents is the writings of:

Figure 2 Sykes Picot Agreement Map; carved up Mesopotamia

- Albert Pike, a known 33ʳᵈ degree freemason who with great detail outlines the three world wars in a published worked dated August 15, 1871: (www.threeworldwars.com/albert-pike.htm)

1. The First World War must be brought about in order to permit the Illuminati to overthrow the power of the Czars in Russia and of making that country a fortress of atheistic Communism. The divergences caused by the "agentur" (agents) of the Illuminati between the British and Germanic Empires will be used to foment this war. At the end of the war, Communism will be built and used in order to destroy the other governments and in order to weaken the religions.

2. "**The Second World War** must be fomented by taking advantage of the differences between the Fascists and the political Zionists. This war must be brought about so that Nazism is destroyed and that the political Zionism be strong enough to institute a sovereign state of Israel in Palestine. During the Second World War, International Communism must become strong enough in order to balance Christendom, which would be then restrained and held in check until the time when we would need it for the final social cataclysm."

3. "**The Third World War** must be fomented by taking advantage of the differences caused by the "agentur"(agents) of the "Illuminati" between the political Zionists and the leaders of Islamic World. The war must be conducted in such a way that Islam (the Muslim Arabic World) and political Zionism (the State of Israel) mutually destroy each other. Meanwhile the other nations, once more divided on this issue will be constrained to fight to the point of complete physical, moral, spiritual and economical

exhaustion...We shall unleash the Nihilists and the atheists, and we shall provoke a formidable social cataclysm which in all its horror will show clearly to the nations the effect of absolute atheism, origin of savagery and of the most bloody turmoil. Then everywhere, the citizens, obliged to defend themselves against the world minority of revolutionaries, will exterminate those destroyers of civilization, and the multitude, disillusioned with Christianity, whose deistic spirits will from that moment be without compass or direction, anxious for an ideal, but without knowing where to render its adoration, will receive the true light through the universal manifestation of the pure doctrine of Lucifer, brought finally out in the public view. This manifestation will result from the general reactionary movement which will follow the destruction of Christianity and atheism, both conquered and exterminated at the same time.

The agenda of #1 was successful; the Russian Revolution took place the following year in October 1917, with the Bolsheviks. These efforts plunged the Soviet state into its dark ages of atheistic values. Communism flourished absorbing surrounding countries westward dividing Germany at Berlin with the well-known "Berlin Wall". Communism did in fact influence for the first time entire nations of atheism... #2 we saw the rise of the political party called the "Nazi Party", which was funded by the Jewish Family Rothschild's...Later the world would witness a mass murder of European Jewish settlers and the rise and fall of Hitler's Germany. This war helped to argue the need of a Jewish state, and collaberately working with the British who had been successful at taking down the Ottoman Caliphate; awarded the Jews stay in Palestine which was already occupied by Arab settlers since the spread of Islam to Jerusalem under the 2ⁿᵈ Caliphate & companion of Nabi Muhammad s.a.w; Omar ibn Al-Khattab r.a. Omar is also the authority who order the erection of the current Mosque called the dome of the Rock, which is the most visible of land marks with its gold rook.. In the After math the United States would grow in its influence balancing the scales of power with the Soviet Communist State until the collapse of the Soviet Union. As I already stated this script has been followed to the letter and the results have been undeniably accurate in keeping the course. This brings us to #3 and the current state of affairs...

What I have share thus far isn't hidden knowledge; instead its prophecy and statements of revelation along with the ability to piece together these information with the politics of the day. I don't credit myself, but instead think of myself also as someone who still growing in understanding. But the average person who thinks of politics separately from that of religious matters; you are doing yourself a huge injustice. The separation of Church from the rule of State effectively gave rise to people being led away from the true nature of political events &

undermining. For politics is another way of saying religion; only difference politics derives from man…

After the 911 event the people initially were driven by emotion to retaliate and united briefly from tragedy. Emotional responses towards anything are not good because often times emotional responses lack reason and more so need no clear evidence in support of the reaction motivated by emotion. This was the people's reaction, and after the emotional speech of President Bush Jr on the grounds of the twin towers the entire country was ready to stand behind him in the name of Justice…Soon the rhetoric of "Weapons of Mass Destruction" began to be heard in every speech and news story. The government now conveniently aligned with the America people, went on to setup campaigns against 7 targeted countries and their governments, the first of which was Iraq.

Figure 3 Retired 4 star General Wesley Clark form commander of NATO Kosovo war 2004

Read the whole interview here: http://www.globalresearch.ca/we-re-going-to-take-out-7-countries-in-5-years-iraq-syria-lebanon-libya-somalia-sudan-iran/5166 "*Democracy Now*"!

March 2, 2007

"We're going to take out seven countries in 5 years, starting with Iraq, and then Syria, Lebanon, Libya, Somalia, Sudan and, finishing off, Iran" —

Now based on what you have read thus far; it concludes perfectly. Take notice also that Iran is the country chosen lastly as it is also the area in which the Ad 'Dajjal will emerge…we are on the cusps of major world events.

Although the bible does contain true information, it also contains many doubtful matters…Along with those doubtful matters, there's also the denying of the last revelation which makes all things clear, explains all things, and brings truth to darkness and falsehood. The cache of knowledge is endless left by the prophet Muhammad s.a.w. and while Christians await the beloved Eisa ibn Mariam A.S. the world steadily becomes more unstable because nothing is done to counter these efforts of evil.

Revelation was given in Hebrew, Aramaic, and Arabic of the last three revelations…just as in language the names of things change, but the thing itself is the same…so is Allah's message…Never has it differed amongst any of the prophets; only differences in language…come to understand this very critical point. Let go of arrogance, societal pressures, family tradition, and or alienation in light of truth…We all answer for ourselves when question by the lord about disobedience and turning from his guidance's; as we also do in this life with daily responsibilities, so why allow anything or anyone to deter you from the truth? They can't save you!!!

R ACISM THE FORGOTTEN TIME BOMB

Deniers of the truth and enemies to humanity are the creators of evil practices that have Broken the spirit and institutionalized people that can longer see freedom, they no longer remember what it looks like, no longer African and have unfortunately succumbed to acceptance of their induce position and status as a people...so why should we expect either of these people to make any changes; the master because he likes the current arrangement or the slave who has lost his will & fight?

Today, black people still petition the government for justice instead of exercising the rights by a unified front. Rioting and burning down your own neighborhoods in frustration then arrested for it and or openly attacked further isn't a condition or an effort that will further your cause nor bring the justice you REQUEST. You see that is the problem; by definition to request something leaves choice to the one being sequestered, and by that same method you have constantly been denied. But let's take a look at the word DEMAND...its fundamentally different and more befitting to the circumstances of African-American peoples in adopting collectively on a unified front.

two-face black leaders who only help to bring about media coverage and stir black emotions of anger; Al Sharpton and the likes will not solve your issues, because they are part of the issue…

When issues arise like the unfortunate case of Travon Martin, what sort of justice is obtained? In my opinion the black community, still divided from hatred of self and expressed in ways of black on black violence, doesn't have the resources to sustain any collective petition they under take. Held to conditions of servitude to jobs or government assistance; we have no collective pool of trusted resources to carry out and exercise our rights. Still too dependent on what falls from masters table; instead of becoming independent and intuitive. Not even the big church figures utilize their FULL pool of resources in aiding this vital purpose; but instead offer the people to turn the other cheek doctrine of accepting oppression which is their purpose and government censorship to do so...

Love of this world, partying and chasing money, cars and women have softened a people who lost the recipe of fight and sacrifice of their ancestry. Look at the Indians against the cowboys of early America, the Haitians in defeating the French, apartied of South Africa, the Palestinians' against Zionism and all us Muslims today who fight and resist the powers who seek to imprison us. Even if you lose or die in the cause...This is an honorable action and it's respected just as much as it is hated. Your lack of respect lies in your loud speech and cowardice...Power only respects power and you must come to this understanding.

Forget about the hype of terrorism and the deliverance of bombs, IED's and conspiracies of sleeper cells waiting to take orders in continuing the terrorization of America...there truly is a sleeper cell that's more or less been Ticking away...far more dangerous than any outside threat and current circumstances and legislation has persisted in pushing the limits. America has militarized its police force and gets a lot of practice in the racial conflicts that have been taking place. A powder keg if you will; and the wick has been shorting over the years with each case of police violence.

With Racial tensions mounting, combined with more poverty from scarce jobs, no public figure has more openly addressed these issues since the sixties...Martin Luther King JR. One approach through organizing and petitioning the government and Malcolm X another still utilizing organization but also incorporating the tactic of taking the rights owed by "any means necessary." Asking the government for something that should've been readily given, was the justification of employing their own means. Besides, the rights that we were ignored the government was also not coming to the aide of black subjects victimized by violence. So, it was now clear to tactfully resist, defend & exercise the justice they sought on their own spearheading the action themselves...

I mean, really how long does someone have to ask for what is rightfully theirs before it's given? Intelligence defines matters of peace as well as matters that outline justified war...*KEEP THIS POINT ON YOUR MIND*

He gave a lot of lectures and also participated in debate in prestigious universities detailing the dissatisfactions and complaints of America's hostage & Captive black population often with standing ovations and deep resonating impressions.

For 12 long years I lived within the narrow minded confines of the straight jacket world created by my strong belief that Elijah Mohammed was a messenger direct from God... and my faith in what I now see to be a pseudo-religious philosophy that he preaches. . . .
I shall never rest until I have undone the harm I did to so many well-meaning, innocent Negroes who... now believe in him even more fanatically and more blindly than I did...
I am not a racist... In the past I permitted myself ... to make sweeping indictments of all white people, the entire white race, and these generalizations have caused injuries to some whites and perhaps did not deserve to hurt. Because of my spiritual enlightenment... as a result of my pilgrimage [to Mecca, Arabia]...
I no longer subscribe to make sweeping indictments of any one race

Never have I witnessed such sincere hospitality and the over-whelming sprit of true brotherhood as is practiced by people of all

Colors and races here [Mecca].... this pilgrimage... has forced me
To re-arrange much of my thought patterns... and toss aside some of
My previous conclusions.... In the words and in the actions and in
The deeds of 'white' Muslims I felt the same sincerity that I felt
Among the black African Muslims of Nigeria, Sudan, and Ghana

"Malcolm X" Malik Al-Hajj Al-Shabazz

But there are powers that be who are at work in the shadows of American consciousness under minding any progress made by the populace in efforts to commit the world to global oneness and control. Take a look at an interesting quote by Mr. Rockefeller from his own book:

"**Memoirs of David Rockefeller**" 2002 soft cover edition page 405 states the following quote:

"for more than century ideological extremists at either end of the political spectrum have seized upon well-publicized incidents...such as my encounter with Castro to attack the Rockefeller family for the inordinate influence they claim we have wielded over the American political and economic institutions. Some even believe we are part of a secret cabal working against the best interests of the United States, characterizing my family and me as internationalists...and conspiring with others around the world to build a more integrated global political and economic structure; one world, if you will. If this is the charge, I stand guilty, and I am proud of it."

Some of these fighting factors against justice are carried out by organizations that people have either no understanding of and or don't understand their true function. One thing is certain, a person cannot serve two masters...many of our politicians are actively holding office while holding alternate memberships to these affiliations. They may say, it's just a membership nothing different from that of your local gym or spa; but I beg to differ that the guilt lies in the affiliation alone. The constitutional law & and position in government is directly violated by their membership, and raise unquestionable doubt to motives or any incentives they might exercise at the fate of the country. Why aren't then the people arguing this case? Have they accepted this condition?

CFR (Counsel on Foreign Relations)

This organization is one of many with a dodgy motives base...you should read up on it; but in the mean-time have a look at some of its members who also share political office now or did in recent past...
In addition, I often ask myself why is a non-governmental organization persisting in foreign affairs?

Well known members who did or still do hold political office:

- Secretary of treasury Timothy Geithner Bilderberg and trilateral commission
- Secretary of state Hillary Clinton Bilderberg, CFR and husband in trilateral commission
- Ambassador to the United Nations Susan Rice trilateral commission
- National security advisor Gen. James L. Jones Bilderberg, CFR & trilateral commission
- Deputy national security advisor Thomas Donilon CFR
- State Department Special Envoy Henry Kissinger Bilderberg, CFR and trilateral commission

- Chairman, economic recovery committee Paul Volcker Bilderberg, CFR & trilateral commission
- Director of national security admiral Dennis C. Blair Bilderberg, CFR & trilateral commission
- Secretary of defense Robert Gates Bilderberg, CFR,& trilateral commission
- Deputy secretary of state James Steinberg Bilderberg, CFR & trilateral commission
- State depart special envoy Richard M. Haass Bilderberg, CFR & president of the trilateral commission
- Presidential advisor Alan Greenspan Bilderberg, CFR, & trilateral commission
- State department special envoy Richard C. Holbrooke Bilderberg, CFR, & trilateral commission

We live in a world prison, but you can't see the bars.

slam vs Nationalism

There is only one America despite all the different depictions used to convince gullible people of a clean image.

Nationalism creates a disconnection of people to the rest of humanity… as far as the nation-state not having set parameters of what defines the people other than land!

Nationalism is an ideology parallel to Islam and the foundation for modern nation-states is built on the concept, idea & principle of loyalty to a country. Many people don't see a problem with being a loyal citizen to a nation-state; it does not clash with one's loyalty to a secularized religion such as Buddhism, Hinduism and Christianity. But it does with Islam….Not because Islam is over inherently political; instead it differs from the others because of its inherent monotheism!!! You see, today most Christians in the West believe that they follow an Abrahamic faith and or tradition; but the reality of the matter is not so. Ignorant to truth that hasn't yet reached them or deniers of truth in Arrogant fashion of family tradition or to what they believe to be socially acceptable; they practice and believe outside of the principals established by Khalil-ul-llah (friend of Allah…Ibrahim) as he is also referred. Western Christianity since its adaption of the Roman Empire in Byzantine…its capital moved from Rome to Constantinople (Istanbul, Turkey today); the emperor Constantine held a counsel in the city of Nicaea in the year 325 A.D. Here he and others mainly Paul who declared himself a follower of Jesus; decided on the traditions and rituals of the Christian faith as it is still practiced today…Constantine himself a pagan of Greek Gods, adopted into the faith paganism…the trinity which has NO proof, the deity of Christ and the likes all solidified into the practices and followed by people who have denied themselves the truth…

For the reason alone, it's easy for the polytheist to accept the idea of loyalties of the highest order to other than god and at the same time to God.

However, for the true monotheist (belief in the oneness of our creator) it's impossible to hold the Creator and other created things on the same level. The Creator alone is above his creation in a manner befitting to his majesty and thus NOTHING can be held in partnership with him. Out of the 5 pillars of Islam

1.   Tawheed- belief in the oneness of the Creator…this is also present in the 1st of the Ten Commandments' but ignored by Christians…hear ye Ol' Israel, the Lord thy God is ONE…

2.   Salah- prayer…five obligatory prayers in remembrance to our creator as fulfillment of the covenant each of us individually have with him…in congregation facing the 1st home of worship built by Ibrahim and his son Isma'il…this uniformity of unity and connection to the whole of humanity. Out of 24hr day, there is always a group in the world throughout its times zones in submission to the creator, which is the definition of Islam…

3. <u>Fasting</u>- obligatory month of Ramadan, which is the month the Qur'an was revealed and also contains Lailtul Qadr (the night of divine decree, which the angels carry out orders of our lord for creation)

4. <u>Zakat (charity)</u> - 2.5% of all wealth given to the poor each year...

5. <u>Hajj</u>- pilgrimage to Mecca...too many virtues to mention...

Under Islam, mankind is one, the land is one, the earth, and all that is given by Allah for life is one and each person has a right and claim to it...the benefit of mankind is regarded and not the benefit of a few...Divine law governs since no man is wiser than the creator, nor are we above it but we ourselves are limited and held as part of creation & also governed by laws of physics & sciences etc. in our own being...

Nationalism calls its subjects of a particular land to come together in loyalty to this land under common cause be it wrong or right and the highest of moral cost from each person. Anything otherwise is regarded treason...But the very essence of Nationalism disregards the wellness of the entire human family. The land created by the Creator is ONE...although it is today divided by oceans, mountains and rivers...it's still one land. When the creator created the land he said to it, "be and it was"; this statement doesn't contain all the many nations 195 I believe that exist today! The land came into existence as one land at one time. Therefore, why does man treat the land differently, with all the imaginary boundaries? How would you actually know if you cross the border of any state, or country if there were not any identifying signs there to tell you? Exactly...!!! You wouldn't! So why do we fall for the asinine idea that nationalism is good or best?

Nationalism is good for dividing and conquering...it's good for claiming resources that lye in a particular area out of greed and not waiting to share...It's born out of Fascism, and Darwinism type ideologies of superiority of one over the other...

So, again...I remind you of your faith & leave you with the question of where in the scripture did any of Allah/God's messengers and prophets ever confirm the rights to such orders amongst mankind? I know some of you with sickness in the heart who still have yet to open it towards reason, may suggest certain verses but I will tell you in advance the next time you are reading scripture pay attention to who is speaking because much of the bible is written in the 3rd person, or for the new testament- Paul is the author...So, you would be wrong in suggesting it's from God or from one of his blessed spirits i.e. Anbiya (Prophets)...

I leave you with the following thoughts and quotes that help to argue my point that nothing should come before Allah/God...

> Our situation today is not so unique to only us Muslims; Catholics and Jews also faced similar issues in the past. In the 1960s, mainstream America was afraid of what it would mean to have John F. Kennedy, a Catholic, as president, just as today we have Fox News trying to scare people

about what it would mean to have Barack Hussein Obama as president. There was fear mongering questioning whether Kennedy would be more loyal to the Vatican or to America.

Sydney E. Ahlstrom, a former professor at Yale, wrote "<u>A Religious History of the American People</u>" in which he spoke about the tension between religious loyalties and nationalistic tendencies. He called it the "American problem" as far back as the 1950s and 60s.

Richard Niebuhr, a theologian and also a former professor at Yale, wrote a book "<u>Christ and Culture</u>" in which he warns that too much loyalty to the state will detract from loyalty to Christ.

Stephen Carter, an African American theologian and a professor at Yale, writes:

I should make my biases clear. I write not only as a Christian but as one who is far more devoted to the survival of my faith — and of religion generally — than to the survival of any state in particular, including the United States of America. I love this nation, with all its weaknesses and occasional horrors, and I cannot imagine living in another one. But my mind is not so clouded with the vapors of patriotism that I place my country before my God. If the country was to force me to a choice — and, increasingly, this nation tends to do that to many religious people — I would unhesitatingly, if not without some sadness for my country, choose my God...

B

RITISH & French POLITICS: Creation of ISRAEL, SAUDI KINGDOM and lands of Mesopotamia

In brief in conclusion to World War!:

The Anglo-French Declaration of November 1918 pledged that Great Britain and France would "assist in the establishment of indigenous Governments and administrations in Syria and Mesopotamia (*meaning the land between the two rivers Euphrates and Tigris*) by "setting up of national governments and administrations deriving their authority from the free exercise of the initiative and choice of the indigenous populations". The French had reluctantly agreed to issue the declaration at the insistence of the British. Minutes of a British War Cabinet meeting reveal that the British had cited the laws of conquest and military occupation to avoid sharing the administration with the French under a civilian regime. The British stressed that the terms of the Anglo-French declaration had superseded the Sykes–Picot Agreement in order to justify fresh negotiations over the allocation of the territories of Syria, Mesopotamia, and Palestine.

On 30 September 1918, supporters of the Arab Revolt in Damascus declared a government loyal to the Sharif of Mecca from the Tribe of Banu Hashem. The Hashemite's were descendant to the Prophet s.a.w… He had been declared 'King of the Arabs' by a handful of religious leaders and other notables in Mecca. On 6 January 1920 Faisal initialed an agreement with Clemenceau which acknowledged 'the right of Syrians to unite to govern themselves as an independent nation' A Pan-Syrian Congress meeting in Damascus had declared an independent state of Syria on the 8th of March 1920. The new state included portions of Syria, Palestine, and northern Mesopotamia. King Faisal was declared the head of State. At the same time Prince Zeid, Faisal's brother, was declared Regent of Mesopotamia.

The San Remo conference was hastily convened. Great Britain and France and Belgium all agreed to recognize the provisional independence of Syria and Mesopotamia, while claiming mandates for their administration. Palestine was composed of the Ottoman administrative districts of southern Syria. Under customary international law, premature recognition of its independence would be a gross affront to the government of the newly declared parent state. It could have been construed as a belligerent act of intervention due to the lack of any League of Nations sanction for the mandates. In any event, its provisional independence was not mentioned, although it continued to be designated as a Class A Mandate.

France had decided to govern Syria directly, and took action to enforce the French Mandate of Syria before the terms had been accepted by the Council of the League of Nations. The French issued an ultimatum and intervened militarily at the Battle of Maysalun in June 1920. They deposed the indigenous Arab government, and removed King Faisal from Damascus in August 1920. Great Britain also appointed a High Commissioner and established their own mandatory regime in Palestine, without first obtaining approval from the Council of the League of Nations, or obtaining the formal cession of the territory from the former sovereign, Turkey.

Attempts to explain the conduct of the Allies were made at the San Remo conference and in the Churchill White Paper of 1922. The White Paper stated the British position that Palestine was part of the excluded areas of "Syria lying to the west of the District of Damascus".

The British Notes taken during a 'Council of Four Conference Held in the Prime Minister's Flat at 23 Rue Nitot, Paris, on Thursday, March 20, 1919, at 3 p.m.' shed further light on the matter. Lord Balfour was in attendance, when Lloyd George explained the history behind the agreements. The notes revealed that:

- '[T]he blue area in which France was "allowed to establish such direct or indirect administration or control as they may desire and as they may think fit to arrange with the Arab State or Confederation of Arab States" did not include Damascus, Homs, Hama, or Aleppo. In area A. France was "prepared to recognise and uphold an independent Arab State or Confederation of Arab States'
- Since the Sykes–Picot Agreement of 1916, the whole mandatory system had been adopted. If a mandate were granted by the League of Nations over these territories, all that France asked was that France should have that part put aside for her.
- Lloyd George said that he could not do that. The League of Nations could not be used for putting aside our bargain with King Hussein. He asked if M. Pichon intended to occupy Damascus with French troops. If he did, it would clearly be a violation of the *Treaty with the Arabs*. M. Pichon said that France had no convention with King Hussein. Lloyd George said that the whole of the agreement of 1916 (Sykes–Picot), was based on a letter from Sir Henry McMahon' to King Hussein.
- Lloyd George, continuing, said that it was on the basis of the above quoted letter that King Hussein had put all his resources into the field which had helped us most materially to win the victory. France had for practical purposes accepted our undertaking to King Hussein in signing the 1916 agreement. This had not been M. Pichon, but his predecessors. He was bound to say that if the British Government now agreed that Damascus, Homs, Hama, and Aleppo should be included in the sphere of direct French influence, they would be breaking faith with the Arabs, and they could not face this.

Lloyd George (Lloyd George's law firm *Lloyd George, Roberts and Co* had been engaged a decade before by the Zionists to work on the Uganda Scheme) was particularly anxious for M. Clemenceau to follow this. The agreement of 1916 had been signed subsequent to the letter to King Hussein. In the following extract from the agreement of 1916 France recognized Arab independence: "It is accordingly understood between the French and British Governments.-(1) That France and Great Britain are prepared to recognize and uphold an independent Arab State or Confederation of Arab States in the areas A. and B. marked on the annexed map under the suzerainty of an Arab Chief." Hence France, by this act, practically recognized our agreement with King Hussein by excluding Damascus, Homs, Hama, and Aleppo from the blue zone of direct administration, for the map attached to the agreement showed that Damascus, Homs, Hama and Aleppo were included, not in the zone of direct administration, but in the independent Arab State. M. Pichon said that this had never been contested, but how could France be bound by an agreement the very existence of which was unknown to her at the time when the 1916 agreement was signed? In the 1916 agreement France had not in any way recognized the Hedjaz. She had undertaken to uphold "an independent Arab State or Confederation of Arab States", but not the King of the Hedjaz. If France was promised a mandate for Syria, she would undertake to do nothing except in agreement with the Arab State or Confederation of States. This is the role which France demanded in Syria. If Great Britain would only promise her good offices, he believed that France could reach an understanding with Feisal.'

T HE RIGHT OF RESISTANCE
(When people understood governance and power)

Today, if you research back in the history of countries that today use their power to colonize and exert power over others, you will almost always find periods in their own histories that speak to the title of this chapter. The Catholics, Jesuits, puritans, and Huguenots all Jockeyed for position in power of one over the other. The dark ages of Europe...different sects of Christianity...

Something I find remarkable are the arguments held between the people back then. Although at differences or in some case rivals and or enemies; the power of reason and eloquent dialogue would often deter advancements or motives until it could be countered in reason or proved fallible. This is a quality that humanity as long since lost, as we are now too sensitive for direct speech, ignorant from lack of knowledge, and unarticulated to communicate effectively. Diplomacy today is persuasive or entrapment by hook or crook...

One of many medieval writings circulated on the order of just rule and tyranny was During France's Protestant past of Huguenots it was outlined in a very influential writing by Stephen Junius Brutus in 1579, seven days after the Saint Bartholomew's massacre were 30,000 people died; "The Defense of Liberty against Tyrants"; written pseudonymously that authority was limited by that of the community as a whole. This particular writing addresses the right of an individual(s) to resist a ruler who was in violation of divine law. However, private citizens must not expel the ruler; instead it is up to the magistrate representing the consensus of the whole to do so...

Two contracts were made one between the ruler and the people, and between the ruler and God. So, if the ruler was witnessed as to having broken either one it was appropriate for his disposal. This particular notion still applies in the laws of ruler ship in God's law from the Quran & Sunnah of Muhammad s.a.w....

You know what one of the biggest, reversed attributes is today, besides the obvious adapted separation of church and state? Western countries predominantly not Muslim, their laws reflect more of the sharia give or take (Arabic for God's law of governance) than Muslim countries themselves. There is more order, more adherence to the law, human and animal rights more or less and cleaner environments all of this due to strict penalties and enforcement primarily. But, this isn't to take into account the idolatry of some in not acknowledgment to the one God alone. It's also a well-known fact that many people were aware of the Quran and its knowledge shared in governance which carries over and confirms earlier books. People like even one of the USA's founding fathers Thomas Jefferson was known to have a Quran in his desk...this explains the open minded, ability to reason, and communicate to a wider audience because they were a well-read age of people who respected knowledge. The constitution when you read it, which maybe you probably never have, is expressed in such a way that protects the rights of people and factors God into the sustenance of daily existence. I beg you, if you haven't to read it over, and while you do reflect upon what you see in your surrounding environments. Surely, you will have to come to the conclusion of awakening to the high-jacking of your government. For non-white readers, yes it's true the constitution wasn't written with the full idea of accepting you as a citizen; but still consider the connotations it employs in conveying its message. Had your full rights been won, and this document followed to the letter and upheld at all cost for not just Americans but also in consideration of humanity, then surely we wouldn't be where we are today.

The lands of Muslims are corrupted, which isn't new news to anyone, and although Muslim latter generations have been taught more about democracy in the light of fun, glitter, and other alluring angles;

Poor and top heavy government suck the wealth upward from what the country produces, so the other public welfare systems suffer as a result.

Which brings me to the idea of a stacked, tier type protection upward that now-a-days is designed to protect the hierarchy by buffering the blow-back that would occur. Like tax structures of corporations, protection is sought in a similar fashion.

One particular key-note that is forgotten due to greed; is the ruler shouldn't allow his/her state to grow beyond the capacity of lost unity. This particular rule of thumb is a vital principle under the system of democracy...unity here is the essence of this governing model & represents cohesion of communication and like-minded ideals reflected in the governance of the government. If the state is allowed to grow past a manageable size, then all of these ideals will not be represented and therefore deteriorate the overall system, mainly in regards to justice. When not all ideas and voices are considered and the whole begins to reflect a decisive few from the collective, you now have effectively committed an injustice to those who are not taken into account. Then, if still allowed to grow, fewer and fewer have their voices represented until you eventually run the risk of complete collapse of unity and in order to maintain peace we find ourselves at the fate of an absolute type power figure I.e. king, emperor, or seized type power utilizing the control of military like tyranny...

The prophet Muhammad s.a.w. said in authentic Hadith (recorded speech) that prophet hood would be followed by caliphs on the prophetic example establishing divine law in the earth since he is the seal of prophet hood. This lasted until the collapse of the Ottomans who were the last to carry the torch of caliphate...

Then it would be followed by kingship (which only a few remain basically to control subjects in the Muslims world and setup by the secular governments who colonized them), then dictatorship which is where we are today...he (s.a.w) went on to say that after dictatorship would be the return of the caliphate (we see this now also in middle east, and although it is fought, it's a promise of our lord to return, so those who fight it are at war with Allah) and then upon return of Esa ibn Mariam a.s (the true messiah, who kills the false one established by the Jews) would be the final return of prophet hood before the last day (end of time)... There are minor and major signs all noted and foretold by Nabi Muhammad s.a.w, marking these events, which all the minor signs have concluded and we are now on the cusps of witnessing the first of the majors signs, which the big war (apocalypse to Christians) starting from Iraq and be a series of small wars everywhere with Muslims would be one of the first. You have to be blind to not see this staring back at you...

After which, like beads on a string, major signs would come one after another 10 in all til the last day...

These prophecies are undeniable truth, and the prophet hood of Muhammad s.a.w. must be acknowledged by those still not familiar although he is written in the Torah, songs of Solomon and gospel. In addition he is also spoken of in the book of Barnabas who was a true disciple of ESA ibn Mariam a.s. but left out of scripture. Ask yourself why in the light of lies and war against Islam; To deny any prophet is to deny them all since their messages of submission to the Lord (which is the meaning of Islam) were all the same worship God alone in truth..."**The Sealed Nectar**" is a very good introduction book about the beloved Prophet Muhammad s.a.w.

In the stages running up to complete tyranny it is now only the elite who benefit and it is only them who are reflected in or above the governance of the lower classes. Sovereignty, if obtained is the absolute and perpetual power of commanding a state; absolute because power it was given without any conditions attached. It's perpetual because it can't be revoked... This is the power of giving orders and taking none. This authority to demand obedience is the ends by which a society will exist nothing else, and all threats are quickly silenced and or imprisoned. In kingdoms especially, the paralleled concept of divine right is used in connection with the kingship in an effort to solidly more the right to the king to rule.

The current King of Morocco is often rumored with words that link him in lineage to the last Prophet Muhammad s.a.w. who was Arab. This couldn't be further from the truth... Nonetheless, there will always be a party who will continue to add these words in the biography of each successive prince in an attempt to legitimize their rule; and unfortunately there will always be a class who are loyal and believe.

In other words they are trying to attach divine appointment so that their position cannot ever be refuted...

In revelation Allah/God himself appoints a king amongst the children of Israel to lead the army...the story appears in the bible but I take it from the Quran which, confirms/abrogates previous revelation:

وقل لهم نبيهم إنّ الله قد بعدي لكم جالوت ملكا قالوا اني يكون له الملك علينا ونحن احقّ بالملك منه و لم يؤت سعة من المال قال أنّ الله اصطفاه عليكم وزاده بسطةً في العم والجسم و الله يؤتي ملكه من يشاء والله واسع علم

"Their prophet said, God has appointed Saul (Talut in Arabic) as a king for you. They replied, "How can he dominate us when we deserve more to be king than he? Besides, he doesn't have abundant wealth." their prophet said, "God has chosen him as your ruler and has given him physical strength and knowledge." god grants his authority to anyone whom he wants, and god is provident and all-knowing.

The reason I bring this particular situation up because it give rise to recent written history...the prophet in during this time in Christian tradition is said to be Samuel. Samuel instructs Saul in divine guidance while he leads the army to fight against the people of Goliath who were occupiers of the land and disbelievers. David who is just a young adolescent defeats Goliath and at the death of Saul and also successor of prophet hood who inherits also the kingship. In my opinion, this kingship has long since set precedence amongst humanity ever since. European countries All had had established kingships, Britain the most visible; the surrounding countries of holy land as the Jews claim it today in there politics and their preparations of the false messiah. It's all relevant to considerations today, and like I've said before it's the disguised religious precedence that is the true agenda culminating today...

After all, what's a Human being to a mob, Mob to a king, King to a god, God to a non-believer who doesn't believe in anything???

F

ALLACIES of DEMOCRACY

Well as I have already mentioned briefly, the size of the state is probably the main killer towards effective democracy. In fact, I find it a bit strange that some of America's closest allies today are kingdoms and tyrannical leaderships, while she herself claims to be a democracy. Why is she not given into encouraging them; her own allies to becoming the same? Non-reflective justices, and secrecy shroud America in hypocrisy towards actively participating with it population in democratic fashion; instead it's as if she is practicing the art of her partners in tyranny and complete control. It's no secret, America's has lost control of her population and the unity as only been adopted in the prefix of being "United" States of America. Because of this lost control you already see the aggression towards subduing the people by revoking constituted rights, evoking dependency economically to jobs, and massive data collection efforts in a pooling movements and affiliations of its citizenry foreign and domestic in anticipation to resistance. Land ownership, and other things that give people independences is now turning into a human herding into mega-cities all over the world.

When I think of democracy, I think of small village living...more ancient than that tribal if you will; self-sufficient and reflective choices of each person. However; although collective thought is promoted in discussion and choice...there is still a leader chosen from amongst them to make final all judgments'. Democratic process of discussion and concerns... but a judgment from one leader which isn't manipulated by another body or hinder; instead such a leader would be entrusted to consider divine law and the over well-fare of the subjects in which he is over...

The democratic model of America is corrupt, and copied off the Roman model. A failed state in its own right by becoming too big and over-extended in its foreign efforts; Americans shouldn't only regard the Romans in the strength of empire in its peak, but should also regard its weaknesses and finally its collapse. This democratic model intended for leadership of a leader but also contains a senate to control or keep the balance of power of the leader from becoming absolute. In here lies the deceit in my opinion...Because like past emperors, whoever controls the military in fact does hold absolute power. Many generals were successful in disposing of emperors by mutiny amongst the ranks of the army and used their influence to overthrow weak leaders. It's really not any different in modern times. As you see, the past couple presidents have widened the use of the military and expanded the military industrial complex...The United States Military today as become a force utilized by mega, international corporations in expanding and protecting vested business interest at the expense of American tax-payer dollars without an agreed upon consensus of the American people unanimously...

Much different than the days of opposing standing armies; the modernity of today's executive branch calls for many managerial tiers all reporting upward to one. The base of the pyramid as expanded with the creation of homeland security etc.

- C.I.A.
- F.B.I.
- SECRET SERVICE
- N.S.A
- D.H.L.S
- ARMY

- MARINES
- NAVY
- AIRFORCE
- NATIONAL GUARD

Each with their own operating budgets, equipment, & personnel it's very hard to manage and to keep the weeds of corruption from taking hold. We all now the each takes orders, but we also know that each has the freedom to do its fair share of dirt when no one is watching.

Conservatives that have debated in the past against big government haven't done much to stop it; and the senate in my opinion carries out votes to appease the people in believing it still functions as it should, but we know well that they have more filibusters' and deadlocked opinions than they do with concluding on important issues. Circle-jerking each other in meaningless speech, often while innocent life are being spent…Isn't anybody else tired of this B.S?

You know, I seen how the government works on the inside, and I see how it works from the outside; I've seen it domestically & I've seen it in foreign affairs…I took responsibility for myself as a human inhabitant on this shared planet with my other fellow human beings black, brown, red, yellow, & white…I came to a conclusion that I wouldn't contribute in any way towards sustaining or being affiliated by citizenship or any or matter what so ever as long as this deliberate behavior is carried out!

I will say it again, Democracy is fundamentally flawed…Civilization that thrived had divine law governing and these laws were upheld at all cost with capital punishment issued toward apostates…This is the action THAT MUST BE TAKEN IN ORDER TO KEEP THE SEEDS OF CORRUPTION FROM BEING PLANTED…THE ABILITY TO DETER CRIME IS BETTER THAN PUNISHMENT FOR CRIMES AFTER THEY ARE COMMITTED…

"So the next time someone asks you, are you with us or against us, there is no simplistic yes and no answer. You answer them as a Muslim, as a proud Muslim and say, I am with you when you do good but I cannot be with you when you do evil and wrong and I will try everything within my legal means to oppose you when you do that wrong. And if this relationship is not acceptable to you, tell me, and I shall leave you, your friendship, your love, your possessions, and if it means leaving the country than so be it, I will leave that as well. But let me tell you, that you shall never find any friend better than someone who expresses his love to you in this manner. You will never find a better citizen than someone whose philosophy is as I have outlined, and you will never find any better brother in faith than someone who helps you when you are right and prevents you when you are wrong"… quote of Yasir Qadhi, from "divided Loyalties"

Modernity vs Simplicity

Castro and Cuba by choice have helped to safeguard their population from corporate disease; Africa, India & Asia also virgin markets that have either by choice or by deliberate setback been safeguarded from the corporate environment of modernity.

Competition is on the path to self-discovery!!! In business it pushes innovation and market fairness...in personal matters it tests our abilities and enables new levels of self-mastery to be reached...

However, the completely corporate existence transforms personal identity into identity of titles...It drives consumption and surplus and ultimately sucks society of its resources and energy leaving only waste. This is not only the model of business but it's also the adaptive behavior of people...nothing is cherished in this type of existence, everything is expendable even life. If this isn't believable then I ask you to look at Sudan, Namibia, South Africa and many other areas that have been disposing life in political rhetoric only to move in corporate entities.

Today greed is the motivation behind all corporate business; bottom-line and bonuses increase the gap between the upper-class and Lower-classes while systematically destroying the middle-class. Since America's induction into the realm of super-powerism and then its successful advance as sole super-power we have witnessed the cycle from agriculture to industrialization and now finally into the credit and finance sector of flipping loans and interest rates.

Now fascist, the government builds wealth on war. Conglomerates granted government contracts to rebuild countries air raided and bombed by the Military. Government coups and high-jacking of mineral wealth in Iraq, Libya, Mahli & Sudan...This is what modernity has brought about. Go figure in the light of technology mankind has degrade in intellect, and has the western world has become addicted to affluent life-styles that actually exploit other human being in 2nd and 3rd world countries.

Legislation & unions that improved working conditions and protected the worker have been destroyed by right-to-work states, and cheaper labor of immigrants, but really it's all been undone by export of manufacturing jobs and lack of innovation in the sciences. To top it all off, there's a decreased middle-class which is known for small business creation.

Speaking of Illegal immigration and those problems that arose in the last decade of severe economy regression since 911... really I don't understand how or why Americans would make it a big issue when they did after decades of silence when work was plentiful...it's hypocritical if you ask me, and quite selfish.

I look at all these situations from the analogy of the sole rich man who lives on the hill...everyday on his way home he drives through the poor areas and at each corner or traffic light people approach his car asking him for whatever it is he can spare. He keeps his windows rolled up to avoid personal contact and keeps his eyes forward or slightly lowered to avoid looking anyone directly in the eye. The rich man owns a conglomerate corporation that has taken all the business from the local people who now suffer from unemployment. Still the people approach the man's car easily with no aggression. Over time their desolation grows more critical and they now run towards the man's car before its come to a complete stop at each traffic light. Begging and turning away from personal pride they throw themselves at the man's mercy for any help, but still he remains cold towards their request....some have made their way now to the man's home where they can see all the delightful foods he's enjoying through the window so they knock and ring the bell, but he still denies their request.

How long do you think this situation will go on before it becomes violent?

We are blessed individually above our means NOT so we can become hoarders...I'm sure most of have heard the term, "you can't take it with you when you die" so why act as such? Inheritances etc. yes that's fine, but surely what is sufficient is enough more tends to corrupt people as Bill Gates and other super-wealthy have turned philanthropist making huge donations of their wealth realizing an inheritance of their estates would corrupt absolutely.

If we learned to see things in the proper perspective we would benefit not only ourselves but our surrounding. Instead we are being tested, with more and also with less. Whether one believes that or not, I guess it is the underlying issue, but the vices that have been exploited to recognizing personal differences of race, nationality, culture, religion has gone viral and has polluted the entire world. If you have more than you need, then you may be meant to be the means of someone else just as your own means came from someone else. No matter the rung on the social ladder, everyone is dependent on each other in making their livelihoods, and that ultimately goes back to the creator who has bestowed those favors upon us not to mention life itself...

On the flip side...simplicity doesn't desire anything more than itself...It hold morals and values higher than the acquisition of material or worldly affairs. It's not completely against the advancements in technology, but what it is against are advancements that harm the overall health of the whole. Profits at the price of human well-fare or harm to the environment are disregard and not pursued. These are admirable traits to have. Simplicity harbors peace, and less complication of daily lives because of the tranquil conditions it offers. Often time's people of simplicity are more self-sufficient than people of modernity who rely heavily on technology and their jobs to sustain life. Farmers for example are much more relaxed...I don't necessarily mean the big farmer who gets government subsidy to provide corn & wheat for millions of potential consumers across the country; but instead I'm referring to the person who has planted for him/herself and nice garden and may also have chickens, livestock and other animals for dairy and meat. Talented in other areas of skills and has found the bliss of simple life. The lack of societal pressures, because he/she is self-reliant on their livelihood... Much of the underdeveloped world is like this! It has only been through the heavily and deliberate campaign of America through the media and access to satellite dishes that these new ideas of westernized living has become an image sought after mainly by the youth. Held back for decades by colonization and other deprivatities; while the carrot of prosperity has been dangling in their faces...but the carrot comes with a large price attached to it.

The way I look at it is opposite to what most people I believe think to be prosperity. Why? Two word...Paper money!!! It's not worth anything! The family who hold land, and animals, is self-sufficient in food etc. is wealthier than the city worker who has a mortgage, car loan both at prohibited interest and makes a salary of $100k. This correlation isn't exact; instead it's only to draw a quick point to understanding. After taxes (*which are also not supposed to be*), and all other expenses the disposable income of a family like this isn't much. Besides that they don't own their home, car, maybe even the furnishings in the home etc. So really any savings they have isn't saving at all...Nonetheless, people have accepted the idea that paper money carries wealth, when in fact it's completely the opposite. Today's money is created out of debt and has no gold of silver backing giving it value as I have mentioned in other parts of the book; so why is it that people chase something that carries no value? Instead, they should be doing the opposite by trading the worthless paper money for things that hold value within themselves like land.

Land can be acquired, if too expensive for one, through large groups of people all pooling their resources because land is the resource that not only holds value; it also is never ending in yielding its benefits.

Celebrity Deaths

Celebrity Deaths

Lady-Princess Diana was going to begin campaigning for the Palestinian cause and this is why she was killed. Ex-MI6 agent Annie Machon (British Intelligence, made popular in James bond movies) made a public statement which confirmed The Princesses plans. This went completely against the house of Windsor (the British royal family) and the deception and masquerading the Israeli government to have such a high level public figure siding against their initiative.

Michael Jackson converted to Islam, his brother Jermaine who has since long been Muslim, was preparing another major world tour, which many believe he was going to make public his becoming Muslim. Michael was unafraid and often used his music to reach his audience about injustices. Victimized and slandered with false accusations and demonized by the black community in America, Michael employed the black population of brazil to film his video "They really don't care about us", Like Diana, the idea of such a prominent figure to exercise his faith would be detrimental towards the negative campaign of Islam...the conspiracy is highlighted by the slap on the wrist of the doctor who stands charged with only a 4 yr. prison system...(this was black on black, not another prejudicially motivated sentencing like O.J.) if that doesn't tell you something I don't know what will.

Other celebrity deaths and deaths of celebrity friends & close family has been nothing other than initiations into the elite order which is satanic. Whitney Houston, Michael Jackson, Kanye West's Mother, Bill Cosby's son, Michael Jordan's father, Princess Diane, Jay Z's nephew, John Travolta's Son...have a look at this particular website, I'm sure you will be no less than amazed...

http://mediaexposed.tumblr.com/post/5885817851/sacrifices

MEDIA, (mainly the entertainment industry)

Dr. Jack Shaheen (professor southern Illinois university) in his latest book "real bad Arab", writes in contrast of viewing over 1000 movies dating back in Hollywood that have helped to vilify the Arab as other ethnic groups have also. The significance of the Arab image is not coincidental. The powers that be knew that the culminating events would find itself at war with the last remaining obstacle and that would be Islam. Read Albert Pikes letter http://www.threeworldwars.com/albert-pike2.htm written in 1859; and you will see just how long ago things were planned and disseminated through his book to fellow masons'...

So, what does this have to do with the Arab? Well, all of the other revelations have been destroyed and the images of prophets hidden or depicted in prejudice manners...although the Muslim population of Arabs is small compared to the whole; but with the Quran and the Arabic it is written in gives imagery to the last prophet and therefore the process of discrediting the Arab through media had long since been used in movies. The Quran was virtually non-existent to the mass population of America until the incidents of 911. I fault the Muslims who have migrated there for better lives, in neglecting their duty of conveying the message. Nonetheless, Allah uses the event of 911 to bring about good from bad; because Islam has been growing rapidly ever since.

Bad images of ethnic groups portrayed...

Best-sellers list of munafiqeen (two-face people) now righting stories and appearing on TV shows bad mouthing Islam and the entire campaign built around that concept keeps people who are tired of the religious jargon and convinced of its origins of controlling people only; ready to cope out in adopting a neutral stance. But let me tell you, being neutral isn't safe nor is it correct. Neutrality is considered to be disbelief rather than it is to true belief. Not researching and understanding fully that in which you are affiliated nor becoming enlightened with the last revelation for yourself then you are blameworthy of negligence in your covenant with the creator. Things don't just magically happen nor is true knowledge gained from just following, you have to become fully engaged in your own personal search for truth and then Insha'Allah (god willing) you will find purpose and with that you will have gained everything.

Until the philosophy which holds one race superior and another Inferior
is finally...
and permanently...
Discredited...
And abandoned....
Everywhere is war...
I say war...

That until there's no longer...
First class and second class citizens of any nation...
Until the colour of a man's skin
Is of no more significance than the colour of his eyes
Me say war...

That until the basic human rights Are equally guaranteed to all, Without regard to race
Dis a war.

That until that day
The dream of lasting peace, World citizenship Rule of international morality
Will remain in but a fleeting illusion to be pursued,
But never attained
Now everywhere is war - war.

And until the ignoble and unhappy regimes
that hold our brothers in Angola, In Mozambique, and South Africa in Sub-human bondage have been
toppled, and
utterly destroyed
well, everywhere is war
me say war...

War in the east,
War in the west,
War up north,
War down south
War - war
Rumours of war.
And until that day,
The African continent
Will not know peace,
We Africans will fight - we find it necessary
And we know we shall win
As we are confident
In the victory

Bob Marley "from is song War"

Ritualistic ceremonies carried out in public view in music award shows, check board floors depicting transcendence of planes of existence, staircases descended in 13 or other symbolic illuminati, Kabbalah mannerisms; while the general public doesn't understand what they're seeing and think of it as entertainment.

The mysticism of this age like previous ages still consist of magic, but there has also been a conditioning to the UFO, alien existence since the emergence of block buster movies like E.T. and others... The concept has virtually made everyone believers in extraterrestrial life. This has no doubt been done to bring an acceptance to the jinn (*who you will read about in next chapters*), which characterizes the Genie and magic lamp; with the advent of the Last Anti-Christ...

T
HE JINN

What do all of the religions of Judaism, Hinduism, and western-Christendom have in common? They are paganistic with worship to different gods. Western-Christendom is derived from astrological signs tied to ancient Egypt and the pagan deities Horus and Isis...these different gods have long been worshiped and best remembered from Egypt depicted as half bird half man, or half dog half man and so on...these shape-shifting being....: *The Messenger of Allah (sal Allahu alaihi wa sallam) said: "The jinn are of three types; one type which flies through the air; one type which is (like) snakes and dogs; and one which moves from place to place." Narrated by Tabaraani.*

For more insight you may also what to read *"**THE WORLD OF JINN AND DEVILS**" by Dr. Umar Sulaiman Al-Ashqar*

I hope I don't speak to far above anyone's understanding or belief, but I will say to you please follow up on the information I share with you for yourself; you will find that these statements are true and have many deep connotation which people need to reconnect with from a spiritual perspective. The use of science and the constant explanations given by man in explaining everything from weather to religion has all been part of a desensitizing of you towards events that will shortly begin to manifest more and more openly. Although many sighting have been recorded, as the turnover of minds and hearts more in acceptance of this new satanic order, more manifestation in areas will occur. Evil has to be the majority and then you will see these beings more openly and more frequently; for our world is off limits to them but they transgress in acceptance of man's worship. Man accepts what he can see and denies the almighty creator who has withheld himself until the day of reckoning...always in control and who is all aware, he doesn't intervene in the will of man nor the jinn whom have chosen volition for themselves. He has defined a term for all things including himself; and That time is running out, soon everyone will see the Lord in the heavens with the angels that carry his throne as well as rows of angels descending in a manner befitting his majesty as we see the sun in its fullness no matter where you stand in this earth....

The people who take the jinn, whom Shaitan is, part, in worship do so because they manifest themselves to these people and have been known to bestow on them special favor and power. People who have gone on record after attending private séance and privileged to see the manifestation of huge beings coming through the wall, speech, levitation, and other unknown powers to man in this world; are convinced by these things of their divinity. The bible omits any knowledge of these beings including their created names, and their abilities. It further omits the ordinance that is upon them to not interfere in the world of the human being. But like ourselves there are some who obey, and others who do not. Also like ourselves there are brigades of believers and non-believers who war against each other as we do in our world over right and wrong.

The Quran and the speech of the prophet as well as prophets before him have tackled these issues and informed people of their existence and warned mankind towards befriending them for worldly favor. Solomon's reign involved the worldly manifestation of them into the world and thus he, Solomon, was given power and control over them. These facts of revelation have been turned into myth and child-like stories of fantasy giving rise to Aladdin and the genie, Sinbad, magic carpets etc...

But the illuminati and others who have access to privileged knowledge of the magic taught during the time of Solomon, and again in Babylon and found by the Templars during the crusades in manuscripts or should I say scrolls buried under the Solomon's palace. This was the real treasure, more so than any jewel blunder...Some of today's Hollywood movies have communicated these messages like "National Treasure", "Lord of the Rings"...

It's real and history is following a script, please learn to pay attention.

Ancient Egypt is highly studied and queried as well as regarded for its tribute to this worship as was also Babylon...Today you find many objects of architecture all resembling Egyptian manna for a recanting and a summoning of this worship in strategic places as well as high energy points in the earth. They see the serpent of Genesis as a light bearer (which is what the name Lucifer means) sharing and enlightening mankind with knowledge by directing him to eat of the tree; thus thee accredit him, Satan the benefactor and hold him praiseworthy أَلُّو بالله من شيطان نر رجيم. There are many, many famous esoteric personalities (*Aleister Crawley, highly regarded and relative to the Bush family*) who have openly written their thoughts and experiences in publishing that have been adapted by elite personalities and doctrines interjected into an occult following. The elite in every age have always been the main ones to reject the revelation of Allah spoken to them by the prophets...

The current concept of Christianity (god dwelling on the inside of his weak human creation, one with god, sons of god, or we are all gods in human garb), Judaism based on the Talmud, Hinduism, Buddhism, Kabbalah, Scientology and so on...these annotations all play off one another and also collaborate efforts to debunked scientific claims of Darwin's evolution and the likes.

The word Muslim is not evil in and of itself as it is seemingly so uttered from the mouths of journalist. The word simply means a person who has submitted themselves to the creator. This action and meaning of the word share no comparison to the image trickery of media.

D OES GOD EXIST
Programmed!!!
Ones and zeros binary coded decimal
Peripheral interface eyes and ears through media channels
Digital screens interpretation

From what's seen and heard repetitively over &over hour on the hour until persuaded to their world view...

Hypnotic notions with deliberate intentions subliminal but proven effective

From radio and syndicated sitcom television shows...

Secularization of the world in degrading education and faithless based religion homage to Sunday worshipers who worship the son...

Chaos ensuing in the midst of completed plans; conformity and acceptance to present day demands...

Engaged in running our mouths, bragging, and showing off buying houses, consuming interest and when you're told about your Lord in truth you say, "Look I have no time for that."

Lips baring witness to what is truly in the heart against you baring witness...

Love for the world, deceived chasing what you believe; heedless of all the signs taking place!

Don't ask any critical questions, concerned now only with filling the belly; affluent lifestyles; days passing quickly running trying to keep pace in the human rat race...

Sold out rebels and political activist of the 1960's revolution
Raised voices
Exercising rights
Today defenders and law makers of the corruption catalyst

Deceivers of reality upholding the illusion to maintain societal cohesion...sustentation of Propagating the Matrixxxxxxx.....

Evolutionist vs creationists' truth over prejudice evil and imperial injustice...

So, how do we know God exists?

Unveiled scenario of a Primordial fire ball, pressurized gases, matter and elements explode....

Set in motion and expanding ever since

GENESIS CONTRADICTIONS HERE

20th century science, collaborative experiments concluding in last revelation while proving the falsehood of what man has written and said was from Allah... The light of truth focused and galvanized, strengthened from decades of denial rough drafting existence in understanding its origins now observed in thermal dynamics & quantum physics...

Just one of the many scientific, perfection of proof within this holy book; Coinciding evidence Words in the Quran Surah Al-Mumeenun (chapter the believer)

"ولقد خلقنا فوق كم سبع طرائق وما كنّا عن الخلق غافلين" and indeed we (we of power) have created above you seven heavens (one over the other), and never are we (we of power) unaware of the creation..."

Long before today, this was understood it was spoken and known from the Quran more than 1400 yrs. ago while most disbelieved or denied its authenticity

Don't repeat the cycle of arrogance by not coming to know this book as well...it's miracles in literary use of the Arabic language and it's accuracies in science are sure to overwhelm you...

Heavens denoted in Arabic as السّماء as'sama meaning literally the expanding skies above and not the heaven as known in the Christian tradition understood to be part of the whole...heaven the paradise is a completely different creation above the lower seven heavens or skies mentioned...

The skies above each with multiple universes each with its own identifying laws & characteristics expanding and disproving the non-expansion theory; the steady state model...

First seen in science by Edward Hubbell in 1929... Like ripples in a pond after a stone is tossed in...Set i motion outward since the initial start.

The center of this world just so happens to be Mecca, Saudi Arabia...more precisely the location of الكعبة the kA'aba...the first house made for worship to the creator.

1st heaven to the 2nd like a ring in a dessert,
2nd to the 3rd like a ring in a dessert,
3rd to the 4th,
4th to the 5th,
5th to the 6th and 6th to the 7th like a ring in a dessert...

The 7th to the Arsh (throne of the creator) like a ring in a dessert...

So He completed them as seven firmaments in two Days and He assigned to each Heaven its duty and command. And We adorned the lower heaven with lights and (provided it) with guard. Such is the Decree of (Him), the Exalted in Might, full of knowledge. [Fussilat 41:12]

It was also narrated that the Prophet told us about one of the angels who carries the 'Arsh. He said that the distance between that angel's ear lobe and his shoulder is equivalent to a seven hundred year journey. [Abu Dawood]

Narrated Al-Abbas ibn Abdul Muttalib
...The heaven which is above it is at a similar distance (going on till he counted seven heavens).

Above the seventh heaven there is a sea, the distance between whose surface and bottom is like that between one heaven and the next... [Sunan of Abu Dawood, Hadith no. 2205]

Narrated Abu Hurayrah
...He then asked, "Do you know what is between you and it?" On their replying that Allah and His Messenger (peace be upon him) knew best, he said, "Between you and it are five hundred years." He then asked, "Do you know what is above that?" On their replying that Allah and His Messenger (peace be upon him) best he said, "Two heavens with a distance of five hundred years between them. He went on speaking like that till he counted seven heavens, the distance between each pair being like between Heaven and Earth. He then asked, "Do you know what is above that?" On their replying that Allah and His Messenger (peace be upon him) knew best, he said, "Above that is the Throne, and the distance between it and the (seventh) heaven is the same as that between each pair of heavens... and nothing is hidden from Allah of your deeds. [Al-Tirmidhi, Hadith no. 1513]

It was said by Neil Armstrong from his orbital experience about the earth, he states, "the earth looks like a hanging sphere" it's oval instead of circular bulging from the point of Mecca. Precisely it is seen to be hanging from the point of the city of Mecca. It was also discovered the earth emits radiation and again the radiation was emanating from Mecca, precisely the Ka'Aba...the radio waves carry out on and on past detection of stopping... This is understood by Muslims from the prophet's speech about hidden knowledge, that each of the celestial bodies (each of the seven heavens) has creation and each also has a house of worship similar to the Ka'Aba on earth. Each is connected ascending all the way up...subhannah Allah (glory be to Allah)....

Einstein's general relativity theory also proved the origin of a beginning in his famous $E=MC^2$ equation, but he introduced something called the cosmological constant 10^{120}

Laws of nature produce no events; instead they are a means of suggesting patterns in which events have occurred and transcended

Like laws of mathematics suggest patterns of transactions as they are intended

For every law states, "if you have "A" and "B" then you can solve for "C"; but you need to acquire two of variables first to find the unknown value X...

Newton himself came to the understanding that his equations of gravity didn't define this force exactly but was a means of tangible notion to

Improbable conclusions of order finely tuned from chaos seen in these evidences substantially reinforced...

What caused the caused that caused the cause that caused the universe??? People Need explanation in doubt of faith

Answered in infinite regress erasing all existence...first domino starts the windfall of all the others no difference with the origin of the universe...

Immaterial, eternal & timeless the concept of Allah's being...

So, Why would an external, infinite, cause bring into existence a finite creation? Allah knows best his own reasons; but the best answer is CHOICE!!! That choice is an indication of a will and will indicate a personality/ intellect.

For those who need more...

The grand design and finger print of the creator...most famously known from the Italian mathematician Leonardo Fibonacci the sequence of numbers with the previous added to get the value of the next 1,1,2,3,5,8,13,21

It's no surprise it's also present in the Quran...

This golden mean ratio is present in ALL creation but let's note some of the plants to start:

1) Elms and plants grow leaves, twigs and branches ½ around the stem
2) Beach tree and plants like it 1/3
3) Oak 2/5
4) Holly 3/8
5) Large trees 5/13

½...,1/3....,2/5....,3/8....,5/13 we see the sequence present

Golden ratio in DNA 34 angstroms long
   21 angstroms wide. =1.618 for each full cycle of its double helix spiral

Present in the heart muscle, bronchial tube branches, electrical potential of neurons and the arrangement of the brains micro-tubials...

Sunflower Florence perfect spirals of 55, 34, 21; of pineapple and pine-comb are the same

Curve of a crashing wave, starfish, pedals of flowers, human construction & symmetry, paintings of art, architecture, and the cosmos 100,000 light years across all depict the same sequence which taken as a ratio gives us the golden mean ratio 1.618

NOT GOLDEN MEAN OF MECCA, & AYAT IN QURAN HERE??? In addition to the previous miracles about Mecca, and the Ka'Aba are:

1) It's the center of the world

2) Zero magnetism, no campuses work

3) People live longer and the blessing of zam zam water

(fountain of youth)

Fine tuning of atomic physics:

1) Gravitational constant G=6, 67428*10^-11 N cm/kg^2

2) Plamcks constant H=6, 606068*10^-34 m^2 kg/s

3) Gas constant R=8, 314472 J/m/kg

4) Faraday constant F=9, 6485309*10^4 C Mol -1

5) Mass of electron M=9, 1096*10^-31 kg

6) Mass of proton M=1.6726*10^-27 kg

7) Mass of neutron M=1.6749*10^-27 kg

8) The Loschmidt constant NCL=2, 6867774*10^25 m^3

9) The charge of electron E=1, 60217646*10^-19 coulombs

10) The Avogadro constant N=6, 02214179 *10^28 Mol -1

11) The Boltzmann constant K=1, 3806503 *10^-23 M^2 kg S^-2 k^-1

12) PI = 3.141592653589793238462

13) The speed of light C=299792458 m/sec

Hence the term constant; these values are tuned and held constant without deviation or our existence would seize...

*Galileo states," mathematics is the language in which the creator has written the universe."

*Alexander Polyakov; Russian mathematician states, "We know that nature is described by the best of all possible mathematics because it derives from God."

Quantum physics and the electron microscope as brought the micro-world into focus to our naked eyes; Quarks, nucleon, atoms, molecules, bio molecular cells, and the cell itself then consciousness and the human upright organism

Carbon the building block to life originates in stars...star dust from exploding stars (NOTE THE PROCESS OF STAR DESTRUCTION) scatter the element far and wide

No chance of coincidence to life from nothing...

But wait... What's this theory of evolution?
Come about by chance from a common ancestor all things are said to have evolved through natural selection

Author, Charles Darwin in 1859 wrote the book, Origin of Species

Materialistic and a philosophy based on hypothesis based solely on observation (Gallopacose Island) without biological proof, or fossil records...

Spontaneous generation...

This would definitely suggest life without purpose, a random act; makes life meaningless...

Since medieval times evolutionist believed a host of ridiculous options about how life came about:

Some such thoughts were that wheat would bring about mice, frogs from mud, and insects from left out meat...

Experiments were concocted to prove these hypotheses, but they all ended in utter failure with NO proof or evidences bridges.

A collection of elements in the correct proportions was also gathered and treated with electrical shock which was thought to bring about a human being...disbelief to the highest power in what revelation has taught us abrogation in succession from the one previous...

The microscope again would be a major tool used to falsify all the claims of evolution. Flies were seen leaving their Larvae on meat left out which later incubated into magnets seen on the meat. A world smaller than the human eye now understood.

Louis Pasteur, Fox & Dose) Origin of Life pg. 4-5
"Can matter organize itself? No! Today there is no circumstance known under which one could affirm that microscopic beings have come into the world without parents resembling themselves."

Stanley Miller, American Chemist, "evolutionist used gases thought to be present at the earliest times of the universe, no such thing nor did it prove anything..."

Ending in failure after failure of experiments...

Alexander Oparin, (Origin of Life pg. 196)

"Unfortunately, the origin of the cell remains the question that is the murkiest of all aspects to the whole theory of evolution."

THE CELL

*critical question: how common or rare are functional sequences (proteins) among all possible combinations of amino acids?

Functional folds of a given length.   Number of sequences of a given length = $1/10^{74}$ An outrageously large number to comprehend...

But two more conditions exist that have to be taken into consideration

1) Amino acids are joined by peptide bonds which are 1 in 2 chances...

2) Amino acids are two types' right & left called isomers, and the left hand isomer is the only one that can be used in building proteins; so it's also a 1 in 2 chance...

These added factors raise the possible combinations to $1/10^{164}$... This number dwarfs considerable other factors known to our existence such as:

1) 10^{80} elementary particles in the universe

2) 10^{16} seconds since the big bang

3) 10^{139} events since the beginning of the universe itself...

Conclusion: NO SERIOUS SCIENTIST THINKS RANDOM CHANCE IS CORRECT NOR DID LIFE COME ABOUT RANDOMLY; INSTEAD THEY ALL COCLUDE THAT THESE FINE TUNING FACTORS POINTS TO INTELLIGENT DESIGN...

A CREATOR!!!

Yet they continue to teach and document the theory of evolution despite all the flops in experiments and proven evidences for creation...

In Darwin's book "Origin of Life" he has a chapter entitled "difficulties of theory".... I find it strikingly appropriate in correlation to the failed attempts of evolution since he writes in this chapter about findings to difficult or unexplainable in his theories...

He himself quotes," if it could be demonstrated that any complex organ existed which could not possibly have been formed by numerous, successive, slight modifications; my theory would absolutely break down"... (Origin of Life pg. 189)

Well, today science is demonstrating much more than Darwin's simple observations and disproving this vastly flawed and false claim of evolution. Doormat in the Quran for many centuries lie evidences in revelation to findings of today's science with more yet still untapped. Many scientists have gone on record as to what science is now able to demonstrate today, but present 1400 hundred years ago with the prophet Muhammad s.a.w. something that the bible was never able to do collaboratively with science.

No fossil records have ever been found by paleontologist to suggest evolution. In fact, fossil records sampled from different sentiments of earth have indicates creation from bacteria to mankind appeared abruptly in different layers with no links whatsoever to associate them with evolution on from the other. Why? Because everything was created that's why!!!

But arrogantly still not accepting defeat re-creationist have focused now on depicting ancient man over fossil remains of both prime mates and old humans...

These images are pure fantasy for NO true depiction can be made with fossil remains alone. These actions are also being done with European Egyptologists in depicting these well-known facts of black people in history with European noses & characteristics...some have even begun to paint over black images to lighten the color in the hieroglyphs.

It's criminal and it's continuing even into modern times as some people are unwilling to ACCEPT the TRUTH!!!

1) Piltdown man 1912 England, by Charles Dawson was the most successful images managing to hold attention for almost 30yrs. Later, when investigators took a second look they found the jaw bone of an arrangatain place on a human skull...Fraud

2) Neanderthal man advanced as evidence in 1856 & dismissed in 1960

3) Zinjanthropus man advanced as evidence in 1912 and dismissed in 1953

4) ramapithecus man advanced as evidence in 1964 and dismissed in 1979

"it seems to me that when confronted with the marvels of life and the universe, one must ask why and not just how. The only possible answers are religious...I find a need for God in the universe and in my own life."

Arthur L. Schawlow
1981 Nobel Prize in Physics

"For the scientist who has lived by his/her faith in the power of reason, the story ends like a bad dream. He has scaled the mountain of ignorance; He is now about to conquer the highest peak; as he pulls himself over the final rock, when he finally reaches the summit, he is greeted by a band of theologians who have been sitting there for centuries"...

Robert Jastron (1925-2008)

Famous American astronomer and physicist who worked for NASA for more than 20yrs.

In Segway to concluding summary, the last two quotes are enormously, huge in regards to science...

It is always easy to see what is real verses that which is fake...

We shall show them Our signs on the horizons and within themselves until it will be manifest to them that it is the Truth. Does your Lord not suffice, since He is Witness over all things?

How! Are they still in doubt about the meeting with their Lord? Is not He surrounding all things? **SURAH FUSSILAT (41:53-54)**

Revelation always can be proved in science because it's absolute truth and more less there for humanity as signs and proof of a creator. Science itself can't be cheated because it is regulated by laws, and the practice of those laws in concluding what revelation has been saying all along.

Revelation is a living document, and the Quran has secrets from its advent to every generation until the last day. Secondly, it is grammatically and linguistically free of any errors; and lastly it is in the language it was reveal and can be read as so...the truth will always stand apart from falsehood...

Religion is about faith; Islam has both FAITH & PROOF...

Anti-Christ...Ad-Dajjal

After all it was the corrupt Jews and Romans who persecuted and accused Jesus; and it's been their collaboration in running the affairs of the world after Jesus until the coming of Muhammad (***peace on both the blessed messengers of Allah***) who re-established the rule of divine law under the golden age of Islam until the fall of the last Caliphate in Turkey on the prophetic model of divine law governance. Nothing coincidental about that!

The red carpet has been rolled out to accept this imposter...a palace has been built in the salt marsh lands outside of Medina, Saudi Arabia exactly as the prophet said, because Ad 'Dajjal is prohibited entrance into Mecca or Medina by Angels that he is able to see. Watch the short clip
www.youtube.com/watch?v=YcmIRx1Kin8

The language of the Quran is in Arabic which is the preserved revelation (*not the translation, translations are to help the non-Arabic speaking person understand Allah's word*) it's in Arabic because Muhammad spoke Arabic, as Musa a.s. The Saudi Kingdom has also gone to great lengths of abolishing the prophet's home, and other land marks of his companions and wives. Architecture all over the world, company logos with hidden ONE-EYED or 666 imagery are present everywhere, and the building up of NATO, and government take-overs of countries all surrounding or posing threat to Israel have been overthrown and held in constant instability from resistance of indigenous people fighting foreign occupation or interference.

All of it is prophesized so; we know today that the Anti-Christ time is near.

All the homosexual cases of priest; which homosexuality is a big ritual in Satanism... If you pay attention you will see all the pyramids and eyes in the designs around the church symbolic for the one-eyed Antichrist that will emerge soon. It's not a game folks...

ESA ibn Mariam will descend from the sky; Dajjal will emerge from Isfahan, Iran...this is another sign that he is not the truth Messiah in which he will claim...

What follow are a collection of ahadith (defined as speech from the blessed prophet's mouth and recorded by creditable companions) They're listed in no particular order and some have taken place, are currently taking place and or have yet to come...If misunderstood, please feel free to email me and or seek the answers from a knowledgeable source...

For those who are still not familiar with the Prophet Muhammad s.a.w I also invite you to read "***The sealed Nectur***". Prophecy from All of Allah's prophets is true and will surely manifest itself at its prescribed time; thus you must bear witness. It's foolish to deny and dreadful to fight, for that would be no different from fighting with Allah/God, because he's the one who sent his blessed spirits i.e. prophets to instruct, give the glad tiding to the just, guide and warn humanity so that we may be successful in acquiring our real home, by obedience in this world...Please have a look and ponder over!

Sahih al-Bukhari "Afflictions and the End of the World"
Narrated Anas bin Malik:

The Prophet said, "Ad-*Dajjal* will come to Medina and find the angels guarding it. So Allah willing, neither Ad-*Dajjal*, nor plague will be able to come near it."

المَدِينَةَ يَأْتِيهَا الدَّجَّالُ، فَيَجِدُ المَلاَئِكَةَ "حَدَّثَنِي يَحْيَى بْنُ مُوسَى، حَدَّثَنَا يَزِيدُ بْنُ هَارُونَ، أَخْبَرَنَا شُعْبَةُ، عَنْ قَتَادَةَ، عَنْ أَنَسِ بْنِ مَالِكٍ، عَنِ النَّبِيِّ صلى الله عليه وسلم قَالَ
يَحْرُسُونَهَا، فَلاَ يَقْرَبُهَا الدَّجَّالُ ـ قَالَ ـ وَلاَ الطَّاعُونَ، إِنْ شَاءَ اللَّهُ

Sahih Muslim the Book Pertaining to the "**Turmoil and Portents of the Last Hour**" (Kitab Al-Fitan wa Ashrat As-Sa'ah)

Anas b. Malik reported that Allah's Messenger (may peace be upon him) said:

There will be no land which would not be covered by the *Dajjal* but Mecca and Medina, and there would no passage out of the passages leading to them which would not be guarded by angels arranged in rows. Then he (the *Dajjal*) would appear in a barren place adjacent to Medina and it would rock three times that every unbeliever and hypocrite would get out of it towards him.

حَدَّثَنِي عَلِيُّ بْنُ حُجْرٍ السَّعْدِيُّ، حَدَّثَنَا الوَلِيدُ بْنُ مُسْلِمٍ، حَدَّثَنِي أَبُو عَمْرٍو، - يَعْنِي الأَوْزَاعِيَّ - عَنْ إِسْحَاقَ بْنِ عَبْدِ اللَّهِ بْنِ أَبِي طَلْحَةَ، حَدَّثَنِي أَنَسُ بْنُ مَالِكٍ، قَالَ قَالَ
لَيْسَ مِنْ بَلَدٍ إِلاَّ سَيَطَؤُهُ الدَّجَّالُ إِلاَّ مَكَّةَ وَالمَدِينَةَ وَلَيْسَ نَقْبٌ مِنْ أَنْقَابِهَا إِلاَّ عَلَيْهِ المَلاَئِكَةُ صَافِّينَ تَحْرُسُهَا فَيَنْزِلُ بِالسَّبَخَةِ فَتَرْجُفُ "رَسُولُ اللَّهِ صلى الله عليه وسلم
"المَدِينَةُ ثَلاَثَ رَجَفَاتٍ يَخْرُجُ إِلَيْهِ مِنْهَا كُلُّ كَافِرٍ وَمُنَافِقٍ .

Sahih al-Bukhari "Virtues of Madinah"
Narrated Abu Sa'id Al-Khudri:

Allah's Apostle told us a long narrative about Ad-*Dajjal*, and among the many things he mentioned, was his saying, "Ad-*Dajjal* will come and it will be forbidden for him to pass through the entrances of Medina. He will land in some of the salty barren areas (outside) Medina; on that day the best man or one of the best men will come up to him and say, 'I testify that you are the same *Dajjal* whose description was given to us by Allah's Apostle.' Ad-*Dajjal* will say to the people, 'If I kill this man and bring him back to life again, will you doubt my claim?' They will say, 'No.' Then Ad-*Dajjal* will kill that man and bring him back to life. That man will say, 'Now I know your reality better than before.' Ad-*Dajjal* will say, 'I want to kill him but I cannot.' "

حَدَّثَنَا يَحْيَى بْنُ بُكَيْرٍ، عَنْ عُقَيْلٍ، حَدَّثَنَا اللَّيْثُ، عَنِ ابْنِ شِهَابٍ، قَالَ أَخْبَرَنِي عُبَيْدُ اللَّهِ بْنُ عَبْدِ اللَّهِ بْنِ عُتْبَةَ، أَنَّ أَبَا سَعِيدٍ الخُدْرِيَّ ـ رضى الله عنه ـ قَالَ حَدَّثَنَا رَسُولُ اللَّهِ
يَأْتِي الدَّجَّالُ، وَهُوَ مُحَرَّمٌ عَلَيْهِ أَنْ يَدْخُلَ نِقَابَ المَدِينَةِ ـ بَعْضَ السِّبَاخِ الَّتِي بِالمَدِينَةِ، فَيَخْرُجُ "صلى الله عليه وسلم حَدِيثًا طَوِيلاً عَنِ الدَّجَّالِ، فَكَانَ فِيمَا حَدَّثَنَا بِهِ أَنْ قَالَ
إِلَيْهِ يَوْمَئِذٍ رَجُلٌ، هُوَ خَيْرُ النَّاسِ ـ أَوْ مِنْ خَيْرِ النَّاسِ ـ فَيَقُولُ أَشْهَدُ أَنَّكَ الدَّجَّالُ، الَّذِي حَدَّثَنَا عَنْكَ رَسُولُ اللَّهِ صلى الله عليه وسلم حَدِيثَهُ، فَيَقُولُ الدَّجَّالُ أَرَأَيْتَ إِنْ قَتَلْتُ
"هَذَا ثُمَّ أَحْيَيْتُهُ، هَلْ تَشُكُّونَ فِي الأَمْرِ فَيَقُولُونَ لاَ. فَيَقْتُلُهُ، ثُمَّ يُحْيِيهِ فَيَقُولُ حِينَ يُحْيِيهِ وَاللَّهِ مَا كُنْتُ قَطُّ أَشَدَّ بَصِيرَةً مِنِّي اليَوْمَ، فَيَقُولُ الدَّجَّالُ أَقْتُلُهُ فَلاَ أُسَلَّطُ عَلَيْهِ .

Sahih Muslim the Book Pertaining to the "**Turmoil and Portents of the Last Hour**" (Kitab Al-Fitan wa Ashrat As-Sa'ah)

Ibn Umar reported that Allah's Messenger (may peace be upon him). made a mention of *Dajjal* in the presence of the people and said: Allah is not one-eyed and behold that *Dajjal* is blind of the right eye and his eye would be like a floating grape.

حَدَّثَنَا أَبُو بَكْرِ بْنُ أَبِي شَيْبَةَ، حَدَّثَنَا أَبُو أُسَامَةَ، وَمُحَمَّدُ بْنُ بِشْرٍ، قَالاَ حَدَّثَنَا عُبَيْدُ، اللَّهِ عَنْ نَافِعٍ، عَنِ ابْنِ عُمَرَ، ح وَحَدَّثَنَا ابْنُ نُمَيْرٍ، - وَاللَّفْظُ لَهُ - حَدَّثَنَا مُحَمَّدُ بْنُ بِشْرٍ،
إِنَّ اللَّهَ تَعَالَى لَيْسَ بِأَعْوَرَ . أَلاَ وَإِنَّ المَسِيحَ الدَّجَّالَ "حَدَّثَنَا عُبَيْدُ اللَّهِ، عَنْ نَافِعٍ، عَنِ ابْنِ عُمَرَ، أَنَّ رَسُولَ اللَّهِ صلى الله عليه وسلم ذَكَرَ الدَّجَّالَ بَيْنَ ظَهْرَانَيِ النَّاسِ فَقَالَ
أَعْوَرُ العَيْنِ اليُمْنَى كَأَنَّ عَيْنَهُ عِنَبَةٌ طَافِيَةٌ

Sahih al-Bukhari "Afflictions and the End of the World"
Narrated Hudhaifa:

The Prophet said about Ad-*Dajjal* that he would have water and fire with him: (what would seem to be) fire, would be cold water and (what would seem to be) water, would be fire.

إِنَّ مَعَهُ مَاءً وَنَارًا، فَنَارُهُ مَاءٌ بَارِدٌ، "حَدَّثَنَا عَبْدَانُ، أَخْبَرَنِي أَبِي، عَنْ شُعْبَةَ، عَنْ عَبْدِ الْمَلِكِ، عَنْ رِبْعِيٍّ، عَنْ حُذَيْفَةَ، عَنِ النَّبِيِّ صلى الله عليه وسلم قال في الدَّجَّالِ قَالَ أَبُو مَسْعُودٍ أَنَا سَمِعْتُهُ مِنْ رَسُولِ اللَّهِ صلى الله عليه وسلم "وَمَاؤُهُ نَارٌ .

Jami' at-Tirmidhi Chapters on Virtues
Narrated Umm Sharik:

That the Messenger of Allah (SAW) said: "The people will flee from the *Dajjal* such that they will go to the mountains." Umm Sharik said: "O Messenger of Allah! Where will the Arabs be that day?" He said: "They will be few."

حَدَّثَنَا مُحَمَّدُ بْنُ يَحْيَى الأَزْدِيُّ، حَدَّثَنَا حَجَّاجُ بْنُ مُحَمَّدٍ، عَنِ ابْنِ جُرَيْجٍ، أَخْبَرَنِي أَبُو الزُّبَيْرِ، أَنَّهُ سَمِعَ جَابِرَ بْنَ عَبْدِ اللَّهِ، يَقُولُ حَدَّثَتْنِي أُمُّ شَرِيكٍ، أَنَّ رَسُولَ اللَّهِ صلى الله عليه وسلم قال " لَيَفِرَّنَّ النَّاسُ مِنَ الدَّجَّالِ حَتَّى يَلْحَقُوا بِالْجِبَالِ " . قَالَتْ أُمُّ شَرِيكٍ يَا رَسُولَ اللَّهِ فَأَيْنَ الْعَرَبُ يَوْمَئِذٍ قَالَ " هُمْ قَلِيلٌ " . قَالَ أَبُو عِيسَى هَذَا حَدِيثٌ حَسَنٌ غَرِيبٌ صَحِيحٌ .

Sunan Abi Dawud "Battles" (Kitab Al-Malahim)

Narrated Abu Hurayrah: The Prophet (saws) said: The Last Hour will not come before there come forth thirty *Dajjals* (fraudulents), everyone presuming himself that he is an apostle of Allah.

لا تَقُومُ السَّاعَةُ "حَدَّثَنَا عَبْدُ اللَّهِ بْنُ مَسْلَمَةَ، حَدَّثَنَا عَبْدُ الْعَزِيزِ، ـ يَعْنِي ابْنَ مُحَمَّدٍ ـ عَنِ الْعَلاَءِ، عَنْ أَبِيهِ، عَنْ أَبِي هُرَيْرَةَ، عَنْ رَسُولِ اللَّهِ صلى الله عليه وسلم حَتَّى يَخْرُجَ ثَلاَثُونَ دَجَّالُونَ كُلُّهُمْ يَزْعُمُ أَنَّهُ رَسُولُ اللَّهِ

Sunan Ibn Majah the Chapters on "Tribulations from Sunan Ibn Majah"
It was narrated from Mu'adh bin Jabal that the Prophet (saw) said: "The great fierce battle, the conquest of Constantinople and the emergence of *Dajjal*, will all happen within seven months."

حَدَّثَنَا هِشَامُ بْنُ عَمَّارٍ، حَدَّثَنَا الْوَلِيدُ بْنُ مُسْلِمٍ، وَإِسْمَاعِيلُ بْنُ عَيَّاشٍ، قَالاَ حَدَّثَنَا أَبُو بَكْرِ بْنُ أَبِي مَرْيَمَ، عَنِ الْوَلِيدِ بْنِ سُفْيَانَ بْنِ أَبِي مَرْيَمَ، عَنْ يَزِيدَ بْنِ قُطَيْبٍ السَّكُونِيِّ، ـ الْمَلْحَمَةُ الْكُبْرَى وَفَتْحُ الْقُسْطَنْطِينِيَّةِ وَخُرُوجُ الدَّجَّالِ فِي سَبْعَةٍ "وَقَالَ الْوَلِيدُ يَزِيدُ بْنُ قُطَيْبَةَ ـ عَنْ أَبِي بَحْرِيَّةَ، عَنْ مُعَاذِ بْنِ جَبَلٍ، عَنِ النَّبِيِّ ـ صلى الله عليه وسلم ـ قَالَ "أَشْهُرٍ .

Sunan Ibn Majah the Chapters on "Tribulations from Sunan Ibn Majah"
It was narrated from 'Abdullah bin Busr that the Messenger of Allah (saw) said: "Between the fierce battle and the conquest of Al-Madinah will be six years, and the appearance of *Dajjal* will come in the seventh."'

بَيْنَ الْمَلْحَمَةِ وَفَتْحِ "حَدَّثَنَا سُوَيْدُ بْنُ سَعِيدٍ، حَدَّثَنَا بَقِيَّةُ، عَنْ بَحِيرِ بْنِ سَعْدٍ، عَنْ خَالِدِ بْنِ أَبِي بِلاَلٍ، عَنْ عَبْدِ اللَّهِ بْنِ بُسْرٍ، قَالَ قَالَ رَسُولُ اللَّهِ ـ صلى الله عليه وسلم ـ "الْمَدِينَةِ سِتُّ سِنِينَ وَيَخْرُجُ الدَّجَّالُ فِي السَّابِعَةِ .

Riyad as-Salihin "The Book of Miscellaneous ahadith of Significant Values"

Abu Sa'id Al-Khudri (May Allah be pleased with him) reported: I heard the Prophet (PBUH) saying, "*Dajjal* (the Antichrist) will come forth and a person from amongst the believers will go towards him and the armed watchmen of *Dajjal* will meet him and they will say to him: 'Where do you intend to go?' He will say: 'I intend to go to this one who has appeared.' They will say to him: 'Don't you believe in our lord (meaning *Dajjal*)?' He will say: 'There (i.e., we know Him to be Allah, Alone, without any partners) is nothing hidden about our Rubb.' Some of them will say: 'Let us kill him', but some others will say: 'Has your lord (*Dajjal*) not forbidden you to kill anyone without his consent?' So they will take him to *Dajjal*. When the believer will see him, he will say: 'O people! This is *Dajjal* about whom the Messenger of Allah (PBUH) has informed us.' *Dajjal* will have him laid on his stomach and have his head. He will be struck on his back and on his stomach. *Dajjal* will ask him: 'Don't you believe in me?' He will say: 'You are the false Messiah.' He will then give his order to have him sawn with a saw into two from the parting of his hair up to his legs. After that *Dajjal* will walk between the two halves and will say to him: 'Stand up', and he will stand on his feet. He will then say to him: 'Don't you believe in me?' The person will say: 'It has added to my insight that you are *Dajjal*.' He will add: 'O people! He will not be able to behave with anyone amongst people in such a manner after me.' *Dajjal* will try to kill him. The space between his neck and collarbone will turn into copper and he will find no way to kill him. So he will catch hold of him by his hand and feet and throw him into (what appears to be the fire). The people will think that he has been thrown into the fire whereas he will be thrown into Jannah." The Messenger of Allah (PBUH) added, "He will be the most eminent amongst the people with regard to martyrdom near the Rubb of the worlds."[Muslim]

- وعن أبي سعيد الخدري رضي الله عنه عن النبي صلى الله عليه وسلم قال: "يخرج الدجال فيتوجه قبله رجل من المؤمنين فيتلقاه المسالح: مسالح الدجال، فيقولون له: إلى أين تعمد؟ فيقول: أعمد إلى هذا الذي خرج فيقولون له أو ما تؤمن بربنا؟ فيقول: ما بربنا خفاء! فيقولون: اقتلوه، فيقول بعضهم لبعض: أليس قد نهاكم ربكم أن تقتلوا أحداً دونه، فينطلقون به إلى الدجال، فإذا رآه المؤمن قال: يا أيها الناس إن هذا الدجال الذي ذكر رسول الله صلى الله عليه وسلم ؛ فيأمر الدجال به فيشبح؛ فيقول: خذوه وشجوه، فيوسع ظهره وبطنه ضرباً، فيقول: أو ما تؤمن بي؟ فيقول: أنت المسيح الكذاب! فيؤمر به ، فيؤشر بالمنشار من مفرقه حتى يفرق بين رجليه، ثم يمشي الدجال بين القطعتين ، ثم يقول له: قم ، فيستوي قائماً، ثم يقول له: أتؤمن بي؟ فيقول: ما ازددت فيك إلا بصيرة، ثم يقول: يا أيها الناس إنه لا يفعل بعدي بأحد من الناس، فيأخذه الدجال ليذبحه، فيجعل الله ما بين رقبته إلى ترقوته نحاساً، فلا يستطيع إليه سبيلاً، فيأخذ بيديه ورجليه فيقذف به، فيحسب الناس أنما قذفه إلى النار ، وإنما ألقي في الجنة" فقال رسول الله صلى الله عليه وسلم : "هذا أعظم الناس شهادة عند رب العالمين" ((رواه مسلم)). وروى البخاري بعضه بمعنى "المساحل" :هم الخفراء والطلائع.

Sahih al-Bukhari "Afflictions and the End of the World"

Narrated Al-Mughira bin Shu'ba: Nobody asked the Prophet as many questions as I asked regarding Ad-*Dajjal*. The Prophet said to me, "What worries you about him?" I said, "Because the people say that he will have a mountain of bread and a river of water with him (i.e. he will have abundance of food and water)" The Prophet said, "Nay, he is too mean to be allowed such a thing by Allah'" (but it is only to test mankind whether they believe in Allah or in Ad-*Dajjal*.)

حدثنا مسدد، حدثنا يحيى، حدثنا إسماعيل، حدثني قيس، قال قال لي المغيرة بن شعبة ما سأل أحد النبي صلى الله عليه وسلم عن الدجال ما سألته وإنه قال لي " ما يضرك منه ". قلت لأنهم يقولون إن معه جبل خبز ونهر ماء. قال " هو أهون على الله من ذلك ".

Sunan Ibn Majah "The Chapters on Tribulations from Sunan Ibn Majah"

It was narrated from Jabir bin Samurah, that Nafi' bin 'Utbah bin Abu Waqqas narrated that the Prophet (saw) said: "You will fight the Arabian Peninsula and victory will be granted by Allah. Then you will fight the Romans and victory will be granted (by Allah). Then you will fight *Dajjal* and victory will be granted (by Allah)." Jabir said: "*Dajjal* will not appear until you have fought the Romans."

حَدَّثَنَا أَبُو بَكْرِ بْنُ أَبِي شَيْبَةَ، حَدَّثَنَا الْحُسَيْنُ بْنُ عَلِيٍّ، عَنْ زَائِدَةَ، عَنْ عَبْدِ الْمَلِكِ بْنِ عُمَيْرٍ، عَنْ جَابِرِ بْنِ سَمُرَةَ، عَنْ نَافِعِ بْنِ عُتْبَةَ بْنِ أَبِي وَقَّاصٍ، عَنِ النَّبِيِّ ـ صلى الله عليه وسلم ـ قَالَ " سَتُقَاتِلُونَ جَزِيرَةَ الْعَرَبِ فَيَفْتَحُهَا اللَّهُ ثُمَّ تُقَاتِلُونَ الرُّومَ فَيَفْتَحُهَا اللَّهُ ثُمَّ تُقَاتِلُونَ الدَّجَّالَ فَيَفْتَحُهَا اللَّهُ " . قَالَ جَابِرٌ فَمَا يَخْرُجُ الدَّجَّالُ حَتَّى تُفْتَحَ الرُّومُ .

Sunan Ibn Majah "The Chapters on Asceticism from Sunan Ibn Majah"

It was narrated that Abu Sa'eed said: "The Messenger of Allah (saw) came out to us when we were discussing *Dajjal* (False Christ) and said: 'Shall I not tell you of that which I fear more for you than *Dajjal?*' We said: 'Yes.' He said: 'Hidden polytheism, when a man stands to pray and makes it look good because he sees a man looking at him.'"

حَدَّثَنَا عَبْدُ اللَّهِ بْنُ سَعِيدٍ، حَدَّثَنَا أَبُو خَالِدٍ الأَحْمَرُ، عَنْ كَثِيرِ بْنِ زَيْدٍ، عَنْ رُبَيْحِ بْنِ عَبْدِ الرَّحْمَنِ بْنِ أَبِي سَعِيدٍ الْخُدْرِيِّ، عَنْ أَبِيهِ، عَنْ أَبِي سَعِيدٍ، قَالَ خَرَجَ عَلَيْنَا رَسُولُ اللَّهِ ـ صلى الله عليه وسلم ـ وَنَحْنُ نَتَذَاكَرُ الْمَسِيحَ الدَّجَّالَ فَقَالَ " أَلاَ أُخْبِرُكُمْ بِمَا هُوَ أَخْوَفُ عَلَيْكُمْ عِنْدِي مِنَ الْمَسِيحِ الدَّجَّالِ " . قَالَ قُلْنَا بَلَى . قَالَ " الشِّرْكُ الْخَفِيُّ أَنْ يَقُومَ الرَّجُلُ يُصَلِّي فَيُزَيِّنُ صَلاَتَهُ لِمَا يَرَى مِنْ نَظَرِ رَجُلٍ " .

Sahih Muslim "The Book Pertaining to the Turmoil and Portents of the Last Hour" (Kitab Al-Fitan wa Ashrat As-Sa'ah)

Abu Sa'id al-Khudri reported Allah's Messenger (may peace be upon him) as saying: The *Dajjal* would come forth and a person from amongst the believers would go towards him and the armed men of the *Dajjal* would meet him and they would say to him: Where do you intend to go? He would say: I intend to go to this one who is coming forth. They would say to him: Don't you believe in our Lord? He would say: There is nothing hidden about our Lord. They would say: Kill him. Then some amongst them would say: Has your master (*Dajjal*) not forbidden you to kill anyone without (his consent)? And so they would take him to the *Dajjal* and when the believer would see him, he would say: O people, he is the Dajjal about whom Allah's Messenger (may peace be upon him) has informed (us). The *Dajjal* would then order for breaking his head and utter (these words): Catch hold of him and break his head. He would be struck even on his back and on his stomach. Then the *Dajjal* would ask him: Don't you believe in me? He would say: You are a false Masih. He would then order him to be torn (into pieces) with a saw from the parting of his hair up to his legs. After that the *Dajjal* would walk between the two pieces. He would then say to him: Stand, and he would stand erect. He would then say to him: Don't you believe in me? And the person would say: It has only added to my insight concerning you (that you are really the *Dajjal*). He would then say: O people, he would not behave with anyone amongst people (in such a manner) after me. The *Dajjal* would try to catch hold of him so that he should kill him (again). The space between his neck and collar bone would be turned into copper and he would find no means to kill him. So he would catch hold of him by his hand and feet and throw him (into the air) and the people would think as if he had been thrown in the Hell-Fire whereas he would be thrown in Paradise. Thereupon Allah's Messenger (may peace be upon him) said: He would be the most eminent amongst persons in regard to martyrdom in the eye of the Lord of the world.

حَدَّثَنِي مُحَمَّدُ بْنُ عَبْدِ اللَّهِ بْنِ قُهْزَاذَ، مِنْ أَهْلِ مَرْوَ حَدَّثَنَا عَبْدُ اللَّهِ بْنُ عُثْمَانَ، عَنْ أَبِي حَمْزَةَ، عَنْ قَيْسِ بْنِ وَهْبٍ، عَنْ أَبِي الْوَدَّاكِ، عَنْ أَبِي سَعِيدٍ الْخُدْرِيِّ، قَالَ قَالَ رَسُولُ اللَّهِ صلى الله عليه وسلم " يَخْرُجُ الدَّجَّالُ فَيَتَوَجَّهُ قِبَلَهُ رَجُلٌ مِنَ الْمُؤْمِنِينَ فَتَلْقَاهُ الْمَسَالِحُ مَسَالِحُ الدَّجَّالِ فَيَقُولُونَ لَهُ أَيْنَ تَعْمِدُ فَيَقُولُ أَعْمِدُ إِلَى هَذَا الَّذِي خَرَجَ ـ قَالَ فَيَنْطَلِقُونَ بِهِ إِلَى الدَّجَّالِ فَإِذَا ـ فَيَقُولُونَ لَهُ أَوَمَا تُؤْمِنُ بِرَبِّنَا فَيَقُولُ مَا بِرَبِّنَا خَفَاءٌ . فَيَقُولُونَ اقْتُلُوهُ . فَيَقُولُ بَعْضُهُمْ لِبَعْضٍ أَلَيْسَ قَدْ نَهَاكُمْ رَبُّكُمْ أَنْ تَقْتُلُوا أَحَدًا دُونَهُ ـ قَالَ فَيَنْطَلِقُونَ بِهِ إِلَى الدَّجَّالِ فَإِذَا رَآهُ الْمُؤْمِنُ قَالَ يَا أَيُّهَا النَّاسُ هَذَا الدَّجَّالُ الَّذِي ذَكَرَ رَسُولُ اللَّهِ صلى الله عليه وسلم قَالَ فَيَأْمُرُ الدَّجَّالُ بِهِ فَيُنْبَجُ فَيَقُولُ خُذُوهُ وَشُجُّوهُ . فَيُوسَعُ ظَهْرُهُ وَبَطْنُهُ ضَرْبًا ـ قَالَ فَيَقُولُ أَوَمَا تُؤْمِنُ بِي فَيَقُولُ أَنْتَ الْمَسِيحُ الْكَذَّابُ . قَالَ ـ فَيُؤْمَرُ بِهِ فَيُؤْشَرُ بِالْمِنْشَارِ مِنْ مَفْرِقِهِ حَتَّى يُفَرَّقَ بَيْنَ رِجْلَيْهِ ـ قَالَ ـ ثُمَّ يَمْشِي الدَّجَّالُ بَيْنَ الْقِطْعَتَيْنِ ثُمَّ ـ فَيَقُولُ لَهُ قُمْ . فَيَسْتَوِي قَائِمًا ـ قَالَ ـ ثُمَّ يَقُولُ لَهُ أَتُؤْمِنُ بِي فَيَقُولُ مَا ازْدَدْتُ ...

Sahih Muslim "The Book of Faith (Kitab Al-Iman)"

It is narrated on the authority of Abu Huraira that the Messenger of Allah (may peace be upon him) observed: When three things appear faith will not benefit one who has not previously believed or has derived no good from his faith: the rising of the sun in its place of setting, the *Dajjal*, and the beast of the earth.

وَحَدَّثَنَا أَبُو بَكْرِ بْنُ أَبِي شَيْبَةَ، وَزُهَيْرُ بْنُ حَرْبٍ، قَالاَ حَدَّثَنَا وَكِيعٌ، ح وَحَدَّثَنِيهِ زُهَيْرُ بْنُ حَرْبٍ، حَدَّثَنَا إِسْحَاقُ بْنُ يُوسُفَ الأَزْرَقُ، جَمِيعًا عَنْ فُضَيْلِ بْنِ غَزْوَانَ، ح ثَلاَثٌ إِذَا "وَاللَّفْظُ لَهُ ـ حَدَّثَنَا ابْنُ فُضَيْلٍ، عَنْ أَبِيهِ، عَنْ أَبِي حَازِمٍ، عَنْ أَبِي هُرَيْرَةَ، قَالَ قَالَ رَسُولُ اللَّهِ صلى الله عليه وسلم ـ وَحَدَّثَنَا أَبُو كُرَيْبٍ، مُحَمَّدُ بْنُ الْعَلاَءِ خَرَجْنَ لاَ يَنْفَعُ نَفْسًا إِيمَانُهَا لَمْ تَكُنْ آمَنَتْ مِنْ قَبْلُ أَوْ كَسَبَتْ فِي إِيمَانِهَا خَيْرًا طُلُوعُ الشَّمْسِ مِنْ مَغْرِبِهَا وَالدَّجَّالُ وَدَابَّةُ الأَرْضِ

Riyad as-Salihin "The Book of Miscellaneous ahadith of Significant Values"

'Imran bin Hussain (May Allah be pleased with them) reported: I heard the Messenger of Allah (PBUH) saying, "Between time of the creation of Adam and the Resurrection Day, there is nothing greater than the mischief of *Dajjal* (the Antichrist)."[Muslim].

- ما بين خلق آدم إلى قيام الساعة أمر "وعن عمران بن حصين رضي الله عنهما قال: سمعت رسول الله صلى الله عليه وسلم يقول: "أكبر من الدجال ((رواه مسلم)).

Sunan an-Nasa'i » "Book of Seeking Refuge with Allah"

It was narrated from Abu Hurairah that: The Messenger of Allah [SAW] used to seek refuge with Allah from five things, saying: "Seek refuge with Allah from the torment of the grave, and from the torment of Hell, and from the trials of life and death, and from the evil of Al-Masihid-*Dajjal*."

أَخْبَرَنَا عَبْدُ الرَّحْمَنِ بْنُ مُحَمَّدٍ، قَالَ حَدَّثَنَا أَبُو دَاوُدَ، قَالَ حَدَّثَنَا شُعْبَةُ، قَالَ أَخْبَرَنِي يَعْلَى بْنُ عَطَاءٍ، قَالَ سَمِعْتُ أَبَا عَلْقَمَةَ، يُحَدِّثُ عَنْ أَبِي هُرَيْرَةَ، أَنَّ رَسُولَ اللَّهِ صلى عُوذُوا بِاللَّهِ مِنْ عَذَابِ الْقَبْرِ وَمِنْ عَذَابِ جَهَنَّمَ وَمِنْ فِتْنَةِ الْمَحْيَا وَالْمَمَاتِ وَمِنْ شَرِّ الْمَسِيحِ الدَّجَّالِ"اللَّهِ عليه وسلم كَانَ يَتَعَوَّذُ مِنْ خَمْسٍ يَقُولُ

Sunan Abi Dawud » "Battles (Kitab Al-Malahim)"

Narrated Imran ibn Husayn: The Prophet (saws) said: Let him who hears of the *Dajjal* (Antichrist) go far from him for I swear by Allah that a man will come to him thinking he is a believer and follow him because of confused ideas roused in him by him.

"حَدَّثَنَا مُوسَى بْنُ إِسْمَاعِيلَ، حَدَّثَنَا جَرِيرٌ، حَدَّثَنَا حُمَيْدُ بْنُ هِلاَلٍ، عَنْ أَبِي الدَّهْمَاءِ، قَالَ سَمِعْتُ عِمْرَانَ بْنَ حُصَيْنٍ، يُحَدِّثُ قَالَ قَالَ رَسُولُ اللَّهِ صلى الله عليه وسلم هَكَذَا قَالَ "مَنْ سَمِعَ بِالدَّجَّالِ فَلْيَنْأَ عَنْهُ فَوَاللَّهِ إِنَّ الرَّجُلَ لَيَأْتِيهِ وَهُوَ يَحْسِبُ أَنَّهُ مُؤْمِنٌ فَيَتَّبِعُهُ بِهِ مِنَ الشُّبُهَاتِ أَوْ لِمَا يُبْعَثُ بِهِ مِنَ الشُّبُهَاتِ

Sahih al-Bukhari » "Prophets"

Narrated 'Abdullah: The Prophet mentioned the Masih Ad-*Dajjal* in front of the people saying, Allah is not one-eyed while Masih Ad-*Dajjal* is blind in the right eye and his eye looks like a bulging out grape. While sleeping near the Ka'ba last night, I saw in my dream a man of brown color the best one can see amongst brown color and his hair was long that it fell between his shoulders. His hair was lank and water was dribbling from his head and he was placing his hands on the shoulders of two men while circumambulating the Ka'ba. I asked, 'Who is this?' They replied, 'This is Jesus, son of Mary.' Behind him I saw a man who had very curly hair and was blind in the right eye, resembling Ibn Qatan (i.e. an infidel) in appearance. He was placing his hands on the shoulders of a person while performing Tawaf around the Ka'ba. I asked, 'Who is this?' They replied, 'The Masih, Ad-*Dajjal*.' "

حَدَّثَنَا إِبْرَاهِيمُ بْنُ الْمُنْذِرِ، حَدَّثَنَا أَبُو ضَمْرَةَ، حَدَّثَنَا مُوسَى، عَنْ نَافِعٍ، عَنْ عَبْدِ اللَّهِ ذَكَرَ النَّبِيُّ صلى الله عليه وسلم يَوْمًا بَيْنَ ظَهْرَىِ النَّاسِ الْمَسِيحَ الدَّجَّالَ، فَقَالَ " إِنَّ اللَّهَ لَيْسَ بِأَعْوَرَ، أَلاَ إِنَّ الْمَسِيحَ الدَّجَّالَ أَعْوَرُ الْعَيْنِ الْيُمْنَى، كَأَنَّ عَيْنَهُ عِنَبَةٌ طَافِيَةٌ " . " وَأَرَانِي اللَّيْلَةَ عِنْدَ الْكَعْبَةِ فِي الْمَنَامِ، فَإِذَا رَجُلٌ آدَمُ كَأَحْسَنِ مَا يُرَى مِنْ أُدْمِ الرِّجَالِ، تَضْرِبُ لِمَّتُهُ بَيْنَ مَنْكِبَيْهِ، رَجِلُ الشَّعْرِ، يَقْطُرُ رَأْسُهُ مَاءً، وَاضِعًا يَدَيْهِ عَلَى مَنْكِبَىْ رَجُلَيْنِ وَهُوَ يَطُوفُ بِالْبَيْتِ، فَقُلْتُ مَنْ هَذَا فَقَالُوا هَذَا الْمَسِيحُ ابْنُ مَرْيَمَ ثُمَّ رَأَيْتُ رَجُلاً وَرَاءَهُ جَعْدًا قَطَطًا أَعْوَرَ عَيْنِ الْيُمْنَى كَأَشْبَهِ مَنْ رَأَيْتُ بِابْنِ قَطَنٍ، وَاضِعًا يَدَيْهِ عَلَى مَنْكِبَىْ رَجُلٍ، يَطُوفُ بِالْبَيْتِ، فَقُلْتُ مَنْ هَذَا قَالُوا الْمَسِيحُ الدَّجَّالُ ". تَابَعَهُ عُبَيْدُ اللَّهِ عَنْ نَافِعٍ

Sahih al-Bukhari "Military Expeditions led by the Prophet (pbuh) (Al-Maghaazi)"

Narrated Ibn 'Umar: We were talking about Hajjat-ul-Wada', while the Prophet was amongst us. We did not know what Hajjat-ul-Wada' signified. The Prophet praised Allah and then mentioned Al-Masih Ad-**Dajjal** and described him extensively, saying, "Allah did not send any prophet but that prophet warned his nation of Al-Masih Ad-**Dajjal**. Noah and the prophets following him warned (their people) of him. He will appear amongst you (O Muhammad's followers), and if it happens that some of his qualities may be hidden from you, but your Lord's State is clear to you and not hidden from you. The Prophet said it thrice. Verily, your Lord is not blind in one eye, while he (i.e. Ad-**Dajjal**) is blind in the right eye which looks like a grape bulging out (of its cluster). No doubt,! Allah has made your blood and your properties sacred to one another like the sanctity of this day of yours, in this town of yours, in this month of yours." The Prophet added: No doubt! Haven't I conveyed Allah's Message to you? " They replied, "Yes," The Prophet said thrice, "O Allah! Be witness for it." The Prophet added, "Woe to you!" (or said), "May Allah be merciful to you! Do not become infidels after me (i.e. my death) by cutting the necks (throats) of one another."

حَدَّثَنَا يَحْيَى بْنُ سُلَيْمَانَ، قَالَ أَخْبَرَنِي ابْنُ وَهْبٍ، قَالَ حَدَّثَنِي عُمَرُ بْنُ مُحَمَّدٍ، أَنَّ أَبَاهُ، حَدَّثَهُ عَنِ ابْنِ عُمَرَ ـ رضى الله عنهما ـ قَالَ كُنَّا نَتَحَدَّثُ بِحَجَّةِ الْوَدَاعِ وَالنَّبِيُّ صلى الله عليه وسلم بَيْنَ أَظْهُرِنَا، وَلاَ نَدْرِي مَا حَجَّةُ الْوَدَاعِ، فَحَمِدَ اللَّهَ وَأَثْنَى عَلَيْهِ ثُمَّ ذَكَرَ الْمَسِيحَ الدَّجَّالَ فَأَطْنَبَ فِي ذِكْرِهِ وَقَالَ " مَا بَعَثَ اللَّهُ مِنْ نَبِيٍّ إِلاَّ أَنْذَرَ أُمَّتَهُ، أَنْذَرَهُ نُوحٌ وَالنَّبِيُّونَ مِنْ بَعْدِهِ، وَإِنَّهُ يَخْرُجُ فِيكُمْ، فَمَا خَفِيَ عَلَيْكُمْ مِنْ شَأْنِهِ فَلَيْسَ يَخْفَى عَلَيْكُمْ أَنَّ رَبَّكُمْ لَيْسَ عَلَى مَا يَخْفَى عَلَيْكُمْ ثَلاَثًا، إِنَّ رَبَّكُمْ لَيْسَ بِأَعْوَرَ، وَإِنَّهُ أَعْوَرُ عَيْنِ الْيُمْنَى، كَأَنَّ عَيْنَهُ عِنَبَةٌ طَافِيَةٌ. " أَلاَ إِنَّ اللَّهَ حَرَّمَ عَلَيْكُمْ دِمَاءَكُمْ وَأَمْوَالَكُمْ، كَحُرْمَةِ هَذَا، فِي بَلَدِكُمْ هَذَا، فِي شَهْرِكُمْ هَذَا، أَلاَ هَلْ بَلَّغْتُ ". قَالُوا نَعَمْ قَالَ " اللَّهُمَّ اشْهَدْ، ثَلاَثًا، وَيْلَكُمْ، أَوْ وَيْحَكُمْ، انْظُرُوا لاَ تَرْجِعُوا بَعْدِي كُفَّارًا، يَضْرِبُ بَعْضُكُمْ رِقَابَ بَعْضٍ ".

Sahih Muslim"The Book Pertaining to the Turmoil and Portents of the Last Hour" (Kitab Al-Fitan wa Ashrat As-Sa'ah)

Tamim Dari came to Allah's Messenger (may peace be upon him) and informed Allah's Messenger (may peace be upon him) that he sailed in an ocean and his ship lost direction and thus landed at an island. They moved about in that land in search of water. There they saw a person who had been pulling his hair. The rest of the hadith is the same. And he (**Dajjal**) said: If I were to be permitted to set out I would have covered all the lands except Taiba. Then Allah's Messenger (may peace be upon him) brought (Tamim Dari) before the public and he narrated to them and said: That is Taiba and that is the **Dajjal**.

وَحَدَّثَنَا الْحَسَنُ بْنُ عَلِيٍّ الْحُلْوَانِيُّ، وَأَحْمَدُ بْنُ عُثْمَانَ النَّوْفَلِيُّ، قَالاَ حَدَّثَنَا وَهْبٌ، بْنُ جَرِيرٍ حَدَّثَنَا أَبِي قَالَ سَمِعْتُ غَيْلاَنَ بْنَ جَرِيرٍ، يُحَدِّثُ عَنِ الشَّعْبِيِّ، عَنْ فَاطِمَةَ بِنْتِ، قَيْسٍ قَالَتْ قَدِمَ عَلَى رَسُولِ اللَّهِ صلى الله عليه وسلم تَمِيمٌ الدَّارِيُّ فَأَخْبَرَ رَسُولَ اللَّهِ صلى الله عليه وسلم أَنَّهُ رَكِبَ الْبَحْرَ فَتَاهَتْ بِهِ سَفِينَتُهُ فَسَقَطَ إِلَى جَزِيرَةٍ فَخَرَجَ إِلَيْهَا يَلْتَمِسُ الْمَاءَ فَلَقِيَ إِنْسَانًا يَجُرُّ شَعَرَهُ. وَاقْتَصَّ الْحَدِيثَ وَقَالَ فِيهِ ثُمَّ قَالَ أَمَا إِنَّهُ لَوْ قَدْ أُذِنَ لِي فِي الْخُرُوجِ قَدْ وَطِئْتُ الْبِلاَدَ كُلَّهَا غَيْرَ طَيْبَةَ. فَأَخْرَجَهُ رَسُولُ اللَّهِ صلى الله عليه وسلم إِلَى النَّاسِ فَحَدَّثَهُمْ قَالَ هَذِهِ طَيْبَةُ وَذَاكَ الدَّجَّالُ

Sahih al-Bukhari » "Military Expeditions led by the Prophet (pbuh) (Al-Maghaazi)"

Narrated Abu Huraira: I have not ceased to like Banu Tamim ever since I heard of three qualities attributed to them by Allah's Apostle (He said): They, out of all my followers, will be the strongest opponent of Ad-**Dajjal**; 'Aisha had a slave-girl from them, and the Prophet told her to manumit her as she was from the descendants of (the Prophet) Ishmael; and, when their Zakat was brought, the Prophet said, "This is the Zakat of my people."

حَدَّثَنِي زُهَيْرُ بْنُ حَرْبٍ، حَدَّثَنَا جَرِيرٌ، عَنْ عُمَارَةَ بْنِ الْقَعْقَاعِ، عَنْ أَبِي زُرْعَةَ، عَنْ أَبِي هُرَيْرَةَ ـ رضى الله عنه ـ قَالَ لاَ أَزَالُ أُحِبُّ بَنِي تَمِيمٍ بَعْدَ ثَلاَثٍ سَمِعْتُهُ مِنْ رَسُولِ اللَّهِ صلى الله عليه وسلم يَقُولُهَا فِيهِمْ " هُمْ أَشَدُّ أُمَّتِي عَلَى الدَّجَّالِ ". وَكَانَتْ فِيهِمْ سَبِيَّةٌ عِنْدَ عَائِشَةَ فَقَالَ " أَعْتِقِيهَا فَإِنَّهَا مِنْ وَلَدِ إِسْمَاعِيلَ ". وَجَاءَتْ صَدَقَتُهُمْ فَقَالَ " هَذِهِ صَدَقَاتُ قَوْمٍ، أَوْ قَوْمِي ".

Sahih al-Bukhari *"Divine Will (Al-Qadar"*

Narrated Ibn 'Umar: The Prophet said to Ibn Saiyad, "I have kept for you a secret." Ibn Saiyad said, "Ad-Dukh." The Prophet said, "Keep quiet, for you cannot go beyond your limits (or you cannot exceed what has been foreordained for you)." On that, 'Umar said (to the Prophet), "Allow me to chop off his neck!" The Prophet said, "Leave him, for if he is he (i.e., Ad-*Dajjal*), then you will not be able to overcome him, and if he is not, then you gain no good by killing him."

حَدَّثَنَا عَلِيُّ بْنُ حَفْصٍ، وَبِشْرُ بْنُ مُحَمَّدٍ، قَالاَ أَخْبَرَنَا عَبْدُ اللَّهِ أَخْبَرَنَا مَعْمَرٌ، عَنِ الزُّهْرِيِّ، عَنْ سَالِمٍ، عَنِ ابْنِ عُمَرَ ـ رضى الله عنهما ـ قَالَ قَالَ النَّبِيُّ صلى الله عليه وسلم لاِبْنِ صَيَّادٍ ‏"‏ خَبَأْتُ لَكَ خَبِيئًا ‏"‏‏.‏ قَالَ الدُّخُّ قَالَ ‏"‏ اخْسَأْ فَلَنْ تَعْدُوَ قَدْرَكَ ‏"‏‏.‏ قَالَ عُمَرُ ائْذَنْ لِي فَأَضْرِبَ عُنُقَهُ‏.‏ قَالَ ‏"‏ دَعْهُ إِنْ يَكُنْ هُوَ فَلاَ تُطِيقُهُ، وَإِنْ لَمْ يَكُنْ هُوَ فَلاَ خَيْرَ لَكَ فِي قَتْلِهِ ‏"‏‏.‏

Sunan an-Nasa'i" *Book of Seeking Refuge with Allah"*

Abu Hurairah said: "I heard the Messenger of Allah [SAW] say: 'Whoever obeys me has obeyed Allah and whoever disobeys me has disobeyed Allah.' And he used to seek refuge from the torment of the grave, the torment of Hell, the trials that may befall the living and the dead, and the tribulation of Al-Masihid-*Dajjal*."

أَخْبَرَنَا مُحَمَّدُ بْنُ بَشَّارٍ، عَنْ مُحَمَّدٍ، وَذَكَرَ، كَلِمَةً مَعْنَاهَا حَدَّثَنَا شُعْبَةُ، عَنْ يَعْلَى بْنِ عَطَاءٍ، قَالَ سَمِعْتُ أَبَا عَلْقَمَةَ الْهَاشِمِيَّ، قَالَ سَمِعْتُ أَبَا هُرَيْرَةَ، قَالَ سَمِعْتُ رَسُولَ اللَّهِ وَكَانَ يَتَعَوَّذُ مِنْ عَذَابِ الْقَبْرِ وَعَذَابِ جَهَنَّمَ وَفِتْنَةِ الأَحْيَاءِ وَالأَمْوَاتِ وَفِتْنَةِ ‏"‏ مَنْ أَطَاعَنِي فَقَدْ أَطَاعَ اللَّهَ وَمَنْ عَصَانِي فَقَدْ عَصَى اللَّهَ ‏"‏ صلى الله عليه وسلم يَقُولُ الْمَسِيحِ الدَّجَّالِ‏.‏

Sunan Abi Dawud » *"Battles (Kitab Al-Malahim)"*

Narrated Mu'adh ibn Jabal: The Prophet (saws) said: The flourishing state of Jerusalem will be when Yathrib is in ruins, the ruined state of Yathrib will be when the great war comes, the outbreak of the great war will be at the conquest of Constantinople and the conquest of Constantinople when the *Dajjal* (Antichrist) comes forth. He (the Prophet) struck his thigh or his shoulder with his hand and said: This is as true as you are here or as you are sitting (meaning Mu'adh ibn Jabal).

حَدَّثَنَا عَبَّاسٌ الْعَنْبَرِيُّ، حَدَّثَنَا هَاشِمُ بْنُ الْقَاسِمِ، حَدَّثَنَا عَبْدُ الرَّحْمَنِ بْنُ ثَابِتِ بْنِ ثَوْبَانَ، عَنْ أَبِيهِ، عَنْ مَكْحُولٍ، عَنْ جُبَيْرِ بْنِ نُفَيْرٍ، عَنْ مَالِكِ بْنِ يُخَامِرَ، عَنْ مُعَاذِ بْنِ جَبَلٍ، قَالَ قَالَ رَسُولُ اللَّهِ صلى الله عليه وسلم ‏"‏ عُمْرَانُ بَيْتِ الْمَقْدِسِ خَرَابُ يَثْرِبَ وَخَرَابُ يَثْرِبَ خُرُوجُ الْمَلْحَمَةِ وَخُرُوجُ الْمَلْحَمَةِ فَتْحُ قُسْطَنْطِينِيَّةَ وَفَتْحُ قُسْطَنْطِينِيَّةَ خُرُوجُ الدَّجَّالِ ‏"‏ ثُمَّ ضَرَبَ بِيَدِهِ عَلَى فَخِذِ الَّذِي حَدَّثَ ـ أَوْ مَنْكِبِهِ ـ ثُمَّ قَالَ ‏"‏ إِنَّ هَذَا لَحَقٌّ كَمَا أَنَّكَ هَا هُنَا أَوْ كَمَا أَنَّكَ قَاعِدٌ ‏"‏‏.‏ يَعْنِي مُعَاذَ بْنَ جَبَلٍ‏.‏

Sahih Muslim » **"The Book Pertaining to the Turmoil and Portents of the Last Hour"** (Kitab Al-Fitan wa Ashrat As-Sa'ah)

Nafi' b. Utba reported: We were with Allah's Messenger (may peace be upon him) in an expedition that there came a people to Allah's Apostle (may peace be upon him) from the direction of the west. They were dressed in woollen clothes and they stood near a hillock and they met him as Allah's Messenger (may peace be upon him) was sitting. I said to myself: Better go to them and stand between him and them that they may not attack him. Then I thought that perhaps there had been going on secret negotiation amongst them. I however, went to them and stood between him and them and I remember four of the words (on that occasion) which I repeat (on the fingers of my hand) that he (Allah's Messenger) said: You will attack Arabia and Allah will enable you to conquer it, then you would attack Persia and He would make you to conquer it. Then you would attack Rome and Allah will enable you to conquer it, then you would attack the *Dajjal* and Allah will enable you to conquer him. Nafi' said: Jabir, we thought that the *Dajjal* would appear after Rome (Syrian territory) would be conquered.

ـ حَدَّثَنَا قُتَيْبَةُ بْنُ سَعِيدٍ، حَدَّثَنَا جَرِيرٌ، عَنْ عَبْدِ الْمَلِكِ بْنِ عُمَيْرٍ، عَنْ جَابِرِ بْنِ سَمُرَةَ، عَنْ نَافِعِ بْنِ عُتْبَةَ، قَالَ كُنَّا مَعَ رَسُولِ اللَّهِ صلى الله عليه وسلم فِي غَزْوَةٍ ـ قَالَ فَأَتَى النَّبِيَّ صلى الله عليه وسلم قَوْمٌ مِنْ قِبَلِ الْمَغْرِبِ عَلَيْهِمْ ثِيَابُ الصُّوفِ فَوَافَقُوهُ عِنْدَ أَكَمَةٍ فَإِنَّهُمْ لَقِيَامٌ لِقِيَامِ رَسُولِ اللَّهِ صلى الله عليه وسلم قَاعِدٌ ـ قَالَ ـ فَقَالَتْ لِي نَفْسِي

تَغْزُونَ جَزِيرَةَ "الَّتِهِم قَثْمَ بَيْنَهُمْ وَبَيْنَهُ لَا يَخْتَالُونَهُ ـ قَالَ ـ ثُمَّ قُلْتُ لَعَلَّهُ نَجِيٌّ مَعَهُمْ . فَأَيْتُهُمْ قَثْتُ بَيْنَهُمْ وَبَيْنَهُ ـ قَالَ ـ فَحَفِظْتُ مِنْهُ أَرْبَعَ كَلِمَاتٍ أَعُدُّهُنَّ فِي يَدِي قَالَ

قَالَ فَقَالَ نَافِعٌ يَا جَابِرُ لَا نَرَى الدَّجَّالَ يَخْرُجُ حَتَّى تُفْتَحَ الرُّومُ ""الْعَرَبِ فَيَفْتَحُهَا اللَّهُ ثُمَّ تَغْزُونَ فَارِسَ فَيَفْتَحُهَا اللَّهُ ثُمَّ تَغْزُونَ الرُّومَ فَيَفْتَحُهَا اللَّهُ ثُمَّ تَغْزُونَ الدَّجَّالَ فَيَفْتَحُهَا اللَّهُ .

Sahih al-Bukhari » "Characteristics of Prayer"

Narrated 'Aisha: (the wife of the Prophet) Allah's Apostle used to invoke Allah in the prayer saying "Allahumma inni a'udhu bika min 'adhabi l-qabr, wa a'udhu bika min fitnati l-masihi d-*dajjal*, wa a'udhu bika min fitnati l-mahya wa fitnati l-mamat. Allahumma inni a'udhu bika mina l-ma'thami wa l-maghram. (O Allah, I seek refuge with You from the punishment of the grave, from the afflictions of the imposter-Messiah, and from the afflictions of life and death. O Allah, I seek refuge with You from sins and from debt)." Somebody said to him, "Why do you so frequently seek refuge with Allah from being in debt?" The Prophet replied, "A person in debt tells lies whenever he speaks, and breaks promises whenever he makes (them)." 'Aisha also narrated: I heard Allah's Apostle in his prayer seeking refuge with Allah from the afflictions of Ad-*Dajjal*.

حَدَّثَنَا أَبُو الْيَمَانِ، قَالَ أَخْبَرَنَا شُعَيْبٌ، عَنِ الزُّهْرِيِّ، قَالَ أَخْبَرَنَا عُرْوَةُ بْنُ الزُّبَيْرِ، عَنْ عَائِشَةَ، زَوْجِ النَّبِيِّ صلى الله عليه وسلم أَخْبَرَتْهُ أَنَّ رَسُولَ اللَّهِ صلى الله عليه وسلم كَانَ يَدْعُو فِي الصَّلَاةِ " اللَّهُمَّ إِنِّي أَعُوذُ بِكَ مِنْ عَذَابِ الْقَبْرِ وَأَعُوذُ بِكَ مِنْ فِتْنَةِ الْمَسِيحِ الدَّجَّالِ، وَأَعُوذُ بِكَ مِنْ فِتْنَةِ الْمَحْيَا وَفِتْنَةِ الْمَمَاتِ، اللَّهُمَّ إِنِّي أَعُوذُ بِكَ مِنَ الْمَأْثَمِ وَالْمَغْرَمِ ". فَقَالَ لَهُ قَائِلٌ مَا أَكْثَرَ مَا تَسْتَعِيذُ مِنَ الْمَغْرَمِ فَقَالَ " إِنَّ الرَّجُلَ إِذَا غَرِمَ حَدَّثَ فَكَذَبَ، وَوَعَدَ فَأَخْلَفَ ". وَعَنِ الزُّهْرِيِّ، قَالَ أَخْبَرَنِي عُرْوَةُ أَنَّ عَائِشَةَ ـ رضى الله عنها ـ قَالَتْ سَمِعْتُ رَسُولَ اللَّهِ صلى الله عليه وسلم يَسْتَعِيذُ فِي صَلَاتِهِ مِنْ فِتْنَةِ الدَّجَّالِ

THE AGE OF FALSE PROPHETS

I name this particular section as such, because it puts me in mindset of what the true essence of what social media and other media portals are for many. I know not everyone uses them in the same mannerism but, the followings of some people hold a lot of weight in influence. The age of information is in full swing, but a lot of information that is circulating is misleading, and with the following of some it's taken literally and this gives definition to my reference of false prophets...

Journalism has many different codes of ethic...facts and honesty; as well as confirmed information should be a very important priority. I have always found and outlet in writing and I have found it to be very therapeutic for myself being the outwardly spoken personality that I am especially when I'm forced to hold my words for lack of physical audience. At other times I enjoy sharing information...I spend most of free time studying and researching different topics and find it appropriate to share; I would even take it a little further a say I find it obligatory to share because of all the misleading things have uncovered. Now, I know many might say who died and made me the new minister of information...? The answer is no one; I have taken it upon myself and my own personal honor as a man & author to share, and in that commitment I have challenged myself to be truthful. Many things I have written, my closest friends and family have yet to read although I share frequently new publishing's or poems about current affairs etc. The attractiveness to the truth isn't always understood & accepted by everyone with different opinions & beliefs, which is what makes us individually unique, so I don't intend to force feed anyone. Instead, I hope to write in a manner that gives an alternate perspective, but derives from the truth. Words carry so much weight and the penalty for the release of weighty words into our existence has very real repercussion. Like ripples of wave in a pond, words dropped carry and linger outwardly to infinite...the heavier the stone dropped the bigger, further, and faster the ripples outward.

Conversations have dwindled to meaningless chatter, gossip, sports and barber/beauty shop floating opinions in most circles...not to say there aren't any more good conversations, but most I have dropped an ear towards have been more or less about self-perceptive in regards to life. Fewer times do you actually run into discussions...I love to find interesting people who feed off of one another and enable the potential of the conversation to grow in depth and insight. However, the many leaders amongst use both public and private have engulfed themselves in the image of what they say...so, in contrast to the truth when it reaches these people they are more than likely to deal with it from an aggressive stance rather than openly accepting the truth. I know many people from all walks of life, and I myself have a pretty well rounded existence and knowledge from study and travel. I have many, many questions as a youth about what was being taught and believed in and at that particular time I wasn't able to find the answers. Of course I asked my mother many questions, many of which even puzzled her and caused her to second guess what she herself had believed. The critical point is ALL things have a history behind them including what you believe, but most people will not take into account those histories' in uncovering and to fully understand what it is they follow. (his-story) behind the items of man's tampering have affected all facets of life, therefore to blindly follow or to accept something that has been passed down from our parents doesn't protect us from lies.

Laziness, arrogance, life-style, or blissful states of self-proclaimed ignorance is usually the culprit behind perpetuated thoughts & beliefs. But, I tell you the truth is there for those who really have a desire to know. Although it may demand of you some changes...its best! To proclaim love for someone or something is to love that person or thing in TRUTH...to love them in falsehood isn't love at all; instead it was something you gave the way you wanted to give it, not the way it was asked of you to give of yourself...

Another subtle fact is the gain or increase aligned with a doctrine that has been manipulated from the start to walk hand & hand with the individual or national increase towards affluence. For think back to the day of the small quaint congregations who gathered to hear good words of patience, enduring in faith and the good ol'reminder of God...but fast forward 30,40,50 yrs. Until today and you have the prosperity doctrines of mega-congregations. This doctrine of materialism has also played right into the hands of corporations all willing standing by to offer things you don't need or already have. But the prohibition of divine law are ignored and or otherwise changed by man...Same sex marriages etc. What of Faith is this madness, and why is it accepted by others? Pardon me; I'm not purposely poking at one particular group, because today innovations of belief in falsehood are coming from everywhere. Many of today's spiritual leaders have built an image and a livelihood the revolves around this doctrine, so in light of truth they have a huge choice to make in reforming themselves publically to admitting they were wrong, something we seen Malcolm X do after his pilgrimage; or in an effort to save face they carry on as such. What a horrible existence to live a lie...I think this is the biggest problem with acceptance; it will literally mean you have to come to terms with truth both publicly and privately, and let's face it, not many people have it in them to step up like that.

I myself don't want any titles nor do I seek any rank or position, nor do I build an image around myself of being someone who doesn't error. I'm a lifelong student of knowledge (talibul ilm) and my writing, as I have mentioned before is to disseminate the truth not lies. To speak out against anything that is wrong in hoping to reprove those around me is the best kind of friend you can have, instead of having someone who will only enable you to further discord and deeper lies this includes topics of personal nature.

But this is just one aspect...the doctrine is what I intend to be the focus. What we hear from other people and read in the books; how many of you after what you are told or read verify what you have gathered in this information? Translations and interpretations will ALWAYS require of you investigation in its validity because of its nature as not being the source. As in a court of law when the prosecution is presenting its cause it must be able to eradicate any doubt in order to win a conviction...This is really no different. With all the many recent, uncovered truths made by scholars within your own faiths admitting to the errors and inconsistencies why is it still ignored? I'm mean really, that to me is quite embarrassing to see and hear the proof presented, undeniably but people still turn away! Shouldn't you study the origin of the book you follow the history of the rituals & celebrated holidays (*which are meant to be* HOLY_DAYS *in paganism*), the influx of paganistic rituals and the source of the entitled books you find therein? All of these particulars have undeniable facts of truth that will clear up any misconceptions you have as well as settle all the ongoing debates...but, these examples are far above throwing rocks or perpetuating meaningless debates; instead this is about coming to terms with the truth...Language the biggest of obstacles; and rules in Semitic language that still apply when reading translation. The fundamental bricks in which these fallacies are built give a justification to the beautified speech and doctrine that sit above ground. Be it as it may, I tell you today that the earth is shaking and those bricks are being rattled apart as the truth is once again being revived.

You see, the dormant mouths of people who know the truth in spreading that truth are to blame in not disseminating that message years prior. The eastern world largely isn't unaware but the western world especially America and more specifically captive ethnic groups inside of her have been cut off and then manipulated in what it was their ancestors knew. Held to only a few traditions left, like jumping the broom in weddings (*which I remember hearing someone say it isn't authentic at all from African tradition, but that of a slave tradition*) and soul food (*which is the most unhealthy way to eat and the way the slaves ate*)…That brings me to a side note; why do American black people still celebrate rituals of slavery? Shouldn't those things be hated and unhealthy ways abandoned; and a reconnection to the true roots be sought? You would think so, but it's not the case; instead they have become adaptive to every other way they have been pushed or forced to accept. Today, it's the MTV culture of fast money, and lifelong parties…Anyway back to topic.

There is however a group who does know the truth, but as the one who wants to protect his/her image, they deny their followers the truth. The modern day pied piper if you will…they will partake of the fire and so will those who blindly followed them. You see, you have a brain, eyes, and ears and skills that if you use them (*which is the intent*) will help you to come to what you don't know. You just have to want it, and you have to allow yourself not to be biased in any way.

The flesh is a substance that must have a deterring discipline over it otherwise it is naturalistically compelled to lowly matters since it itself is made of the lowly material of dirt in the lowest of the 7 sammawat (*skies or heavens*).

DO AS YOU LIKE PHILOSOPHY VS DISCIPLINED EXISTENCE
Thanks to the insightful questions and conversations of my nephew Aaron; I'm able to attribute something to him as well as share with you. I'm very proud of him and how he has grown up; this is a living example of speaking children at a young age in more meaningful and colorful speech, and not in condescending manners in which we are judging their level of understanding. Children are sponges and ready to learn, adults just need to learn how to capture and keep their attention. Stimulating them keeps them hungry for more. Adults who are in the charge of young people have to realize that you can also be taught, so the traffic flowing with opens two-lanes instead of one.

My nephew ask me," so, what do you think about this uncle? Foreigners who come to America practice their culture in America I.e. dress, religion, food, language etc.; so what about Americans who go to other countries...shouldn't they two be able to practice their culture?"

Pretty, basic question if you're thinking is just scratching the surface; but for me it profound in many ways and it's the derivative to a lot of problems we see today.

I responded in this manner:

America itself is a melting pot of cultures and ethnicities; people from all walks of life...however when people come to America with strict cultural backgrounds America tends to water that culture down, especially for the 2nd generations that will be born there and successively so for latter generations. In the past, When most American's thought of culture they think of food and or language that was primarily the extent. Why? States and cities of diversity have boundaries and neighborhoods that have been largely segregated. America is without culture herself...and if you consider the foundations of the constitutions and the first European settlers we're in search of finding a land in which they would be FREE to DO AS THEY LIKE especially in matters of religion, which is why they were fleeing. A state derived on the notion of liberty in choices no matter the religious connotation of being wrong or right. I support that statement with the following:

"U.S. Treaty No. 122, "The Treaty of Tripoli," Clause 11
As the government of the United States of America is **not** in any sense founded on the Christian religion as it has in itself no character of enmity against the laws, religion or tranquility of Musselmen (*Common English mis-spelling of Muslimmeen (meaning all Muslims)*)...it is declared by the parties that no pretext arising from religious opinions shall ever produce an interruption of the harmony existing between the two countries. (*This treaty was negotiated under George Washington's Administration; and President John Adams, Second U.S. President, submitted it to the U.S. Senate; the 5th U.S. Congress unanimously ratified the treaty; and President Adams signed it on June 5, 1797*).

George Washington First U.S. President

(http://www.adl.org/assets/pdf/civil-rights/religiousfreedom/PORF-StatsFF.pdf

George Washington himself a Freemason, is confirming the fact of absence of religion in laws and establishment of the early republic of America.

Another added proof and a more profound writings (in my opinion) of Thomas Jefferson; The third president, author of the "**Virginia Statue for Religious Freedom**" (1779), said upon rejecting the insertion of the words Jesus Christ into the bill, *"...that [the writers] meant to comprehend, within the mantle of its protection, the Jew and the Gentile, the Christian and Mohammedan, the Hindu and Infidel of every denomination."* All people were to be accommodated.

Paraphrasing Thomas Jefferson in his first inaugural address, he said, *"Let us make sure that as we establish this republic, and as we banish from this land the religious intolerance that we were so accustomed to back home, let us make sure that we do not replace that religious intolerance with a political one."*

These words capture my expression I believe in totality, and hold their own weight in gold. Furthermore, the words and ideas are a far cry to the actions of American leadership today...

American culture use to be pride in innovation, hard work, accomplishment, American enterprise, family and apple pie...these were the good days after World War 2 and America's emergence as a super power. The transition from agriculture to industrialization and sciences...higher education and the American dream. But really, what is the bottom line here in regards to culture? Even in these great times of prosperity America internally was still undergoing sustained tensions from the times of her foundations. The culture wasn't cohesion of the people; instead it was centered around prosperity.

The Grand American Dream as is it still package & sold today...indebted with no intentions of concluding its debt obligation, and collapse internally of education, science, and manufacturing has shifted the countries brand to individual brands. Celebrities, musicians, actors, and athletes all help to sustain an American Idolized image and this is the culture. Millions of people around the world all copying and following such people. Despite the person's character, morals or beliefs people eagerly mimic these people in behavior, dress, speech, and attitudes. This trendsetter/ trend following philosophy of copying someone else is deceitful and dangerous. Culture, this is the culture for American kids: jocks, band, academics, Goth's, stoner's, and outcast Brave souls not inclined to following, but their bravery is usually torture by the others with bullying and other means. Even amongst the young adults and adults; titles and corporate affiliations, clubs, memberships, a-list, v.i.p etc. all superficial means of culturally imposed trends of setting a course for weak minded people to follow along.

This is not freedom at all; instead it is a type of slavery that seemingly appears to have very strong chains and influences amongst the people enslaved. Their uniform of appearance all looks the same, speech the same, attitudes, and thinking all altered and assimilated to those groups. Societal pressures and their pursuit in obedience are the best ways of sustaining your own unfulfilling contentment.

This is where the rubber meets the road...

So, considering this type of culture compared to a culture that is rooted in the higher spiritual consideration of following prophetic examples and mothers of faith like Mariam (Mary mother of Jesus), Khadijah, Fatima, & A'siA (wife of pharaoh, who raised Moses, and who was later killed by pharaoh for her belief)...these cultures are not inspired to follow mankind and the fallacies of human beings in acceptance and glorification but, instead influence people to transcend to higher levels of self-mastery and exemplification to break cultural chains of wrong doing.

In the Quran surah al-araf ayat 157: Allah the most high says: الذين يتبعون الرسول النبي الأمي الذي يجدو نه مكتوبًا عندهم في التوراة و الإنجيل يأمرهم بالمعروف و ينهاهم عن المنكر و يحلّ لهم الطيبات و يحرم عليهم الخبائث و يضع عنهم أسرهم و الأغلال التي كانت عليهم فالذين امنوا به و عزّروه و نصروه و أتبعوا النّور الذي انزل معه او لـئك هم المفلحون those who follow the messenger, the illiterate prophet who is describe in their own books: the Torah and the Gospel which are with them...he will enjoin on them that which is right and forbid them from that which is wrong. He will make lawful for them all pure, good things and prohibit for them only that which is foul & evil; and he will relieve them of their heavy burden and fetters that they used to wear. Then those who believe in him and honor him and help him and follow the light which is sent down with him (the guidance of the Quran): they are the successful...

This particular verses speaks directly to this particular day and age which is succumbed to societal and cultural pressures. He will relieve them of their heavy burdens and fetters...this is literally the burdens of pressures that are surrounding people in their choices and persuasiveness to follow and the fetters are literally the chains & shackles around the hands, feet, and necks of those who follow to those they follow. Yoked together in burden & wrong doing... The implications of this are huge and we must really pay attention to this. Trendsetters and those glorified in their actions, positions, talents, stature, wealth etc. be it they possess something well liked or desirable, the ignorance lies in the blind following them. Not only does a person suffer for their own sin, they will also suffer a portion of the sins of those that followed or they encouraged. Celebrities and the likes and even parents, who have allowed disobedience and wrong doing (although culturally accepted), They have set a trend that will inheritantly convict them and chain themselves too even longer after they are dead with successive generations who adhere and further in deviance. These are the implications of this powerful message. The Quran is known by many other names; two such names as al-furqan (the criterion between wrong and right), and Keetab-ul-nur (book of light) point out the power and references relayed upon the prophet in speech which he spoke to the people...lifting them (the people of Arabia) his people from the ignorance's then of traditional cultural practices. This same light of guidance would eventually spread to the four corners of the world with its laws and a divine blessing if adhered too and so, while it was practiced in the world the world flourished under its promised blessing. Never has the world advanced as it did during the time of expanding libraries and studies of the Quran and Hadith of the prophet s.a.w.

Now we find ourselves at the diminished state of human intellect again and animalistic type servitude towards desires which has made the life of doing as you please something that is cherished by those given into that notion. Addictive in some regards from a lustful state, and constant chase of excitement; While on the flip side appears to be something boring and to strict. Depravity of life itself...but when you view this life as paradise or the only one to live then you will have this attitude. It's a huge misapplication of what freedom really is and they have enslaved themselves with the wrong idea about life. They have lost the understanding of what this life is meant to be a test for all of us in our truth towards faith and to see who truly deserves the abode of the eternal home.

Surah ash-shura ayat 20 من كان يريد حرث الأخرة نزد له في حرث و من كان يريد حرث الدّنيا نئته منها و ما له في الأجرة من نسيب. "Whosoever desires the harvest of the life after, we give him increase in its harvest. And whosoever desireth the harvest of this world, we give him a portion of it, and he hath no portion of the life hereafter..."

انّها هذه الحية الدنية جنّة الطكفر و سجنا المومنين Inna hathahee hayatul Dunya jannatul kafir Wa signul munineen..."verily this worldly life is a paradise for the disbeliever and a prison to the believer..."; words of the blessed prophet/messenger Muhammed s.a.w.

But now, post 911, all this attention on the Middle East and negative imagery has now opened the door for people to pay more attention now to dress, religion, and closer attention to language and businesses in these neighborhoods. Americanized generations both within America and outside of America who have apostated from their beliefs now help in the smirr campaign of the absolute truth in the divine book and guidance trying to keep mankind on a destructive course of consummation. Live TV coverage, interviews, debates and book signings giving their one sided approach and hatred. None of these people have formal education in Islam and others have been victimized by culture in their respective countries and not Islam itself for the true teachings of Islam liberate from every injustice known to man... In predominantly Muslim countries the propaganda is at its worse, and the nightmare of the American dream is ever more colorful while dangling over the head of teenaged youth with opportunities to migrate. Many of the Muslim countries have been deprived of international business as a sort of punishment of faith and world dominance, but with the world wide campaign of expanding NATO in the wake of the major world war, leaders have been conhersed to open their doors to foreign investors and this new boom of economic growth especially in electronic gadgets is being used to convince the youth especially in ways toward modernity as being good even at the cost of their modesty & faith...the American model is good...but you and i both know what they don't know! We understand the corporatized existence pushes consummation until the wealth is gone then it moves on to other virgin areas to repeat its only mission.

Most people in this part of the world haven't been privileged with international travel, nor is their understanding of politics universal and conceptual to the whole, especially to the deceitful cover ups and two-way diplomacy of conglomerates like the USA. Therefore, their naïveté over takes them and they are literally taken advantage of.

American foreign policy for immigration with countries America has interest...

The contrast of cultures are extremely opposite where one is rooted in truth, fairness, modesty and divine adherence...the other is modeled on dis-belief and glorification of self, celebrity, wealth and consummation and the justified means of lying, cheating, stealing, killing etc. to obtain it. Completely at different ends of the spectrum...

But the irony of it for me is how does a person's appearance bother anyone? Don't we individually have a choice as to what we wear within the lines of decencies? Long, short hair, bald head, mustache, beard, clean shaven...clothing of your choice???

In the garb of the hijab it baffles me that although nuns of old and every depiction of Mariam is in the same manner; it's hated because of negative, cultural refutation to the uniform of dressing less for women.; It's as if God has a prescribed time for remembrance and during this time religious or modest attire is ok...Like god seizes to exist during the week when the self is no longer in a mindset of remembering the creator and now carrying out its own will. But for the other culture the thought and connection to Allah never ends...the time for modesty and appropriate manners and action is all the time. Therefore there could never been a complete mesh of these two cultures in my opinion, although patience is exercised in allot cases... In the Muslim world it's tolerated with tourism but words of extreme discomfort and dislike for this are whispered amongst onlookers especially around visited mosques...

the strength of countries in the world influence the opinions of right and wrong based on their position...modernity is seen as progression where modesty and simpler means are seen as primitive and oppressive. The Amish in northeast America have adapted simpler means in their lifestyle as well as beards and women have similar dress too, but spared the bad press they are virtually left to a trouble free non-existence. But, ask you to reconsider deeply any notions you may have in this regard, with the slow decline of American superiority...the buzz on Facebook and other outlets shares openly the collective ideals of a generation tired of American bureaucracy and it is patiently awaiting the further decline and decay of a western system in influencing their respective countries.

The world now defeated in man-made systems of governance (dictators', capitalism, communism, socialism, fascism...and every other ism...), has fallen and we are now back on cultural regions of likeness with the strongest strings being that of religion. It is by this relevance of my nephew's simple question that brings light to past motives up to current events; This cultural conflict is the current campaign undergoing to win hearts and minds to obedience of self-servitude (Satanism) verse obedience to the creator.

This particular adaptation to the added attribution of divinity and or part of the godhead to Esa ibn Mariam a.s is what I personally feel appeals to Christians in allowing themselves to have their cake and eat it too. As I stated before we cannot serve two masters (in this case our desires and The Creator together) we will eventually disobey one to obey another and vice-a-versa; faith and obedience to the creator has to be the goal and desires have to be subdued by working on own selves to come into proper alignment with what is permissible given in the books of our creator to abide by. This is the effort needed for a person to attain higher spiritual levels...We don't get in shape by taking magical pills, wishful thinking spoken aloud while still firmly planted on the couch...or lose wait by diet alone...it takes work...So, how does anyone expect to enter heaven by words professing something first and foremost that aren't true and then secondly by that utterance alone, having no work attributed to it? This is equivalent to catching someone in a blatant lie...because that's what it is...If they were to live forever with this personal belief, never would they ever intend to do right by what they utter i.e. the goal being to leave off prohibited things, truly trying to repent from sin (association of partners in worship of created things, people, fornication, adultery, gambling, interest, drinking, cursing god, lies etc., etc., etc...But instead they would continue living as they please. True Faith would eliminate arrogance and encourage acceptance to hard core facts and also lead people to consideration of all of the books of OUR RABB (LORD) as he has sent his guidance in session to mankind...do not allow bad press or what is societally accepted to alter what you concur to without yourself having investigated the truth. You wouldn't allow bad press or society to keep you from taking a high paying job from a corrupted company; so why gamble with your soul? This is the ultimate fate and uncovering of what they hide behind in this particular declaration of faith...

R eligion

So here we are back where we began...you know why? Because it's always been about religion that's why? You see, the manipulators of recent history let's say the last 1500 yrs. have been following something long ago set in motion. The problem is that they have done such a good job at deceiving the people, hiding information, changing history and disseminating that information through slavery, coloniallisation and miseducation the mindset of the world's people is quite different. The biggest inferiority complex that has carried over is the "skin color" philosophy. The lit-mist test of the "brown paper bag" and anything darker than that is bad is still in effect. The cultural attacks of Christianity in the last 40-50 yrs. have been amazingly effective.

In America the small Baptist churches that where packed every Sunday are long gone and are now over coasted by mega-church structures. But is the doctrine correct? Have any of you really taken the time to research and study what it is you believe? Isn't your soul worth the time and effort to truly know what is being taught and what isn't being taught? There are enough Christian scholars out there who are honest about the faith, themselves long been deceived prior to their own efforts then deeper studies. History also points a big finger at the creation and conception of the western faith (Christianity) especially which came into acceptance by Constantine (the Byzantine Empire, eastern roman empire, today modern day Istanbul).

What is the bible? What are the Torah, Psalms, Songs/Proverbs and Gospel...? Aren't they revaluations given to noble messenger/prophets of God? Musa, David, Solomon, and Jesus? But ask yourself a simple common sense question...did these prophets exist at the same time? With the exception of David and Solomon his son...all these noble men existed hundreds of years apart and each of their books wasn't a compilation like it is today, nor was it in English or any other language except the language of that prophet it was given. It's a simple analysis, but effective and correct. Therefore, you have to come to the startling conclusion that the bible is not from God... It is from man. Each one of these prophets was given A BOOK their respective books of revelation/guidance...they were not given the bible. Those previous books have been lost. This brings us to the rebuttal that what the bible contains is still revelation; but again I say to you where is the original text to confirm that response?

I will however, say that the Quran does confirm many things and in other cases it abrogates information that was lost or not known at all. This is what every revelation has done, confirm and bear witness to what came prior. As the blessed Nabi Esa ibn Mariam a.s stated," he will come and he will confirm me" and that is exactly what Muhammad s.a.w. has done... I don't mention this to slander one while trying to promote the other. Frankly, we Muslims believe the Quran is ultimate truth; therefore it can't be compared to anything in the world...

The succession of revelation is a witness against mankind as to having Allah/God's word while it also unfolds in wisdoms and modernity to mankind. Accepted or denied it will bear witness for or against humanity...protected as promised until the last day in the Arabic language it remains unchanged and uncontested. Allah knows his creation best and knows the evils of history and mankind in quest of power and control... Therefore, there is no excuse for any of us to drop out in using our personal intelligence in searching and learning what has been hidden from us. Many people just boldly deny something based solely on public opinion, but I ask you why?

Are there any free thinking minds anymore? Or has mankind become a collective super-organism in the realm of thinking? Super isn't necessary an adjective towards grandness, but on the contrary it gives reflective reference to the old joke (no intentional degradation intended) , " how many Pollock's does it take to screw in a light bulb?"

Wrong belief and practices are the same as disbelief and each of us has the major responsibility of fulfilling the covenant between ourselves and our creator, to learning the truth about of Lord. Why is this the case? Allah knows the hearts of his creation, he knows what you love, what you're willing to do and what you're not, he knows why you do what you do, and most of all what you truly believe. For faith is manifested in action...leaving off prohibited things and submitting oneself entirely. It's easy for the one with true faith and difficult for those who without.

if someone wishes to remain hopeful in suggestive words of intercession for your soul by just words alone of professing upon "Jesus" words that have be taken for one-line facts and not for literary content and meaning, then that is very dangerous gamble that you are making. In ARABIC i have referenced verses from the Quran...the Arabic , Aramaic, & Hebrew language are very rich and powerful with different structure, and conciseness and unlike English one verse is precise in meaning when the lord is making a point; and in longer stories or con joining thoughts he carries out the speech to multiple verse. I mention this to save you the rebuttal against also using one verse against me. This is also why I list the verse in both languages so you see the differences in length and then maybe from that you understand this point more clearly. The Quran is revelation but it is also a living miracle...but to get its miracle you have to understand the Arabic its self...this is truly the prize for humanity when you come to understand these like billions of others have. Picture witnessing one of the miracles of Jesus or Moses, what would this do to your faith? Probably increase it 100 times over yes? Well, understanding the Quran in Arabic you experience these miracles one after another many of which science is catching up too today like i have previously mentioned. The guidance is exact and amazing...and the miracles are life changing and confirming of faith in Allah subhannahu wa Ta'Ala...

For verily the burden of sins will be paid by the owner of those sins.

There is no excuse of blind following or acceptance of information without careful confirmation. In Islam...We have both faith and proof...

You have to free your minds from the societal traps and then exercise it regularly...once the path of truth is regained it's easy to keep its course; the hard part is making the effort of finding it...

يومئذ و ما لكم من نكير لربّكم مّن قبل ان يأتي يوم لا مردّ له من اللّه ما لكم من ملجاء استجابوا answer the call of your lord before there cometh a day unto you from Allah a day which there is no averting (death). Ye have no refuge on that day, nor have ye any (power of) refusal...

C itations:

I invite you to read a more in-depth analysis...*"Where does the truth Begin"* much of the same research carried over here, with application of more personal topics...

Also "**the traveler**" about societal pressures; and my writing *"Fear"*, addressing some of the induced societal fears upon the public...

Renowned bible scholar Prof. Bart D Ehrman Professor of religious studies at the University of North Carolina at Chapel Hill...

www.adl.org

www.Sunnah.com for prophetic teachings, and authentic documented speech of Prophet Muhammad s.a.w...

اسماعيل

www.ingramcontent.com/pod-product-compliance
Lightning Source LLC
Chambersburg PA
CBHW040320010626
45792CB00024B/2076